Introduction

The history of the United States of America starts with a temporary geological feature, an extensive land bridge created by a drop in sea level during the Wisconsin glacial period of the most recent Ice Age. This exposed land mass, crossing the strait that links Northern Asia with North America, allowed nomadic hunter-gatherers to cross from Siberia to Alaska. Over time, the ice caps receded, the sea level rose again, and the land bridge disappeared from view. The nomads who remained on the Alaskan side became the indigenous peoples of America—the Native Americans.

Thousands of years later, in 1492, the Italian explorer Christopher Columbus set out on his momentous westward voyage across the Atlantic, bound for the "Indies," as Asia was then known. He stumbled quite by accident upon a completely new world. From that moment, a succession of explorers were drawn to the region, each one making new discoveries to add to a growing understanding of its potential for settlement. Within little more than a century, settlers from Spain, England, Holland, and France had established colonies and made them profitable. Despite the trials and tribulations experienced by the settlers, the draw of the New World continued to prove irresistible to many.

The French-American author J. Hector St. John de Crèvecoeur (1735–1813) summed up the energizing effect of this exciting land when he wrote: ". . . Here individuals of all nations are melted into a new race of men, whose labours and posterity will one day cause great changes in the world. . . ."

The *Time Chart of American History* outlines in graphic form the development of the United States from its origins as a vast, empty continent to the vibrant, multicultural land of the twenty-first century. Following the horizontal line from any given date in the vertical chronology puts into context the events and figures in the key areas of Expansion, Conflict, Politics, Economy, Culture, and World Influence that have shaped the modern United States, while additional streams introduce at the relevant point the subjects that underpin or reflect that evolution—the long-standing issues of slavery and the African American civil rights movement, the Native American civil rights movement, and the more recent gay rights movement; development of the military forces and space exploration; and the cultural influences of religion, literature and art, sports, and movies and music.

The accompanying essays present a brief introduction to the most important eras and events in America's history. Although the essays are presented in chronological order, each one explains the historical context and, where relevant, the global context and long-term outcome—so, for example, the essay on the Native Americans spans the period from their arrival on the North American subcontinent to the modern day, while the Western Expansion essay explains the circumstances that at first prevented and then facilitated the fledgling United States' settlement of the continent from "sea to shining sea"—from the Atlantic to the Pacific.

July 4, 1776, the date upon which the Second Continental Congress signed the Declaration of Independence and gave birth to the United States of America, is famed around the world. It is commemorated in many ways, none more symbolic than the Declaration itself, which today is preserved, along with the Constitution and the Bill of Rights, in the Rotunda for the Charters of Freedom in The National Archives Museum in Washington, D.C. A close second in terms of symbolism is the Statue of Liberty that stands, holding her beckoning gold flame aloft, at the entrance to New York Harbor. Presented by France on the centenary of American independence, the statue welcomed the millions of immigrants who arrived by sea in the late nineteenth and early twentieth century, and today continues to inspire with her message of freedom and democracy—of the right of every American, and of people throughout the world, to Life, Liberty, and the Pursuit of Happiness.

NATIVE AMERICANS

Between the end of the last Ice Age—around 20,000 years ago—and the arrival of the European explorers, indigenous peoples populated the lands that would become the United States, migrating as far as South America and, when the ice caps retreated, spreading north into Canada. By the early centuries of the common era, some groups had learned to domesticate and irrigate many of today's familiar food crops—corn, potatoes, squash, and beans. The Ancestral Pueblo, for example, was a successful farming civilization in Southwest America c. 100–1600 C.E.; in addition to crop production, they domesticated dogs to assist with hunting and turkeys for their meat and feathers, and are also noted for their basketry and pottery.

Stuccoed ceramic Hohokam vessel from 600–900 C.E. found in Casa Grande, Arizona.

The reference to the indigenous peoples as "Indians" derives from the Columbus Letter, in which the explorer wrote: "The first island I discovered I gave the name of San Salvador. . . . The Indians call it Guanaham." Of the natives themselves, Columbus wrote, "They are . . . so generous with what they possess, that no one who had not seen it would believe it. . . . They . . . show so much love that they would give their very hearts." It was not long, however, before the natives recognized the explorers and colonists as invaders to be feared, and responded accordingly with hostility.

Estimates of the pre-Columbian Native American population vary widely; what is certain, however, is that

Bird's-eye view of Serpent Mound, the largest serpent effigy in the world, located in Ohio.

the colonists introduced diseases such as smallpox, against which the natives had no resistance—some tribes were annihilated, and others considerably weakened. The Europeans also used strong liquor as a form of currency when trading with the natives, which had a pernicious effect on a population familiar only with mild fermented beverages. Intertribal alliances were forged to promote survival and to resist both the colonists and other, stronger tribes; the natives also soon saw the wisdom of forging alliances and trading partnerships with the colonists, most famously the 1621 peace treaty between the Plymouth colony and the Wampanoag, who shared the first Thanksgiving feast.

From 1640 to 1701 the Iroquois Confederacy, formed around 1600 from five tribes across upper New York state, were involved in the Beaver Wars with the Algonquian-speaking tribes of the Great Lakes region. Beaver pelts were vital currency in trade with the European settlers and the Iroquois wished both to extend their own territories, where beaver was becoming scarce, and to monopolize trading activity. Armed with guns received from Dutch settlers in exchange for pelts, they destroyed several large opposing tribes in violent battles. A further complication was that both the British and French—allied with the Iroquois and Algonquin respectively—wished to monopolize the fur trade between the colonies and Europe. The wars ended in triumph for the British, who now held all trading rights and privileges. Native Americans also participated in all four of the major conflicts between the French and British for control of the colonial territory—King William's War (1689–97), Queen Anne's War (1702–13), King George's War (1744–48), and finally the French and Indian War (1754–63) that resulted in British victory.

Meanwhile, the Native Americans were staging rebellions, triggered in protest at the harsh treatment inflicted on them by the colonists. The 1655 Peach Tree War, for example, erupted when a Dutch settler shot a native woman for stealing a peach from his land—the last straw after years of abuse. Other conflicts broke out as the settlers gained confidence in their wilderness survival techniques and began to push out into Native American territory. King Philip's War (1675–76) was fought between New England settlers and a confederation of tribes including the Wampanoag, who had taught the settlers the very skills that enabled their territorial expansion. The defeat of the confederation indicated the shape of things to come as the British became more ruthless—for example, bounties were awarded for "scalping" the natives, while in 1763 troops besieged during Pontiac's rebellion spread smallpox among the Indians via infected blankets.

The historian Francis Parkman (1823–93) wrote that "Spanish civilization crushed the Indian; English civilization scorned and neglected him; and the French embraced and cherished him." When the French lost their claim to lands in North America to the British, the natives in turn lost the support of the French. Initially, under the 1763 Royal Proclamation, lands north and west of the Appalachian Mountains were declared an Indian reserve and closed to colonial settlement. However, the colonists soon began to ignore the Proclamation Line—and independence from Britain was imminent, after which they could do as they wished without interference from the British government. The Northwest Ordinances (1784, 1785, 1787) allowed for legitimate westward expansion by the admission of new states rather than the expansion of existing states. In response, several tribes formed a confederacy and began a series of raids to discourage settlement, resulting in the Northwest Indian War (1785–95) in which they were eventually defeated.

The Indian Removal Act (1830) led to large-scale removal of the Native Americans from their traditional lands to an area within borders later established by the Indian Intercourse Act (1834). Many perished on the journey; the relocation of the Five Civilized Tribes is known as "the Trail of Tears" for that reason. The Indian Appropriation Act (1851) authorized the creation of the first Indian reservations and a second Act, in 1871, declared that "no Indian nation or tribe within the territory of the United States shall be acknowledged or recognized as an independent nation, tribe, or power. . . ."

The "Reservation Era" (1871–1928) was a period of enforced assimilation. The reservations were often located in dry-climate areas, making self-sufficiency impossible. The Bureau of Indian Affairs, established in 1824, assumed responsibility for the reservations, including the provision of food. The 1880 Civilization Regulations outlawed Indian religions, the practices of medicine men, sacred ceremonies such as the Sun Dance, and even leaving the reservation without permission; offenders were prosecuted in the Courts of Indian Offenses, established in 1883. The Dawes Act (1887) allowed the federal government to sell tribal lands to settlers, and Indian children were removed from their tribal homes and placed in government-run boarding and Christian mission schools.

In 1889, Wovoka, a Paiute mystic, announced the imminent restoration of the Native American way of life, to be brought about by a ritual Ghost Dance that would return the ancestors from the dead. The white colonists would

The Indian Girl's Home depicts a group of Native American girls and Native American police at Big Foot's village on a reservation.

disappear, the sacred lands be returned, and buffalo would once again roam the plains. Buffalo played a key role in the life of the Indians, who used every part of the animal, letting no part of its sacrifice be in vain. Between 1840 and 1885, however, settlers slaughtered the herds; an Army general observed that "[the buffalo hunters] have done more . . . to settle the vexed Indian question, than the entire regular army has done in thirty years."

Ironically, the Ghost Dance cult indirectly expedited the demise of the Native American way of life. The Sioux Wars (1851–90) stemmed from the Fort Laramie treaties of 1851 and 1868, which established vast territorial land rights for the Sioux and "absolute and undisturbed use of the Great Sioux Reservation." However, both treaties were violated, the first by the government and the second by emigrants en route to gold fields in the Black Hills of Dakota. In 1875, the Sioux refused to discuss a proposed government purchase of the Black Hills. Early in 1876, the War Department authorized a round-up of "hostile Sioux" who had failed to report for a head count. The resulting hostilities culminated in the Battle of Little Bighorn—Custer's Last Stand—on June 25, when the Sioux

A Sioux painting on an animal hide depicts the Battle of Little Bighorn, also known as General Custer's Last Stand, with Native American warriors and U.S. Army soldiers.

Tatonka-I-Yatanka, also known as Sitting Bull, was a chief and holy man of the Hunkpapa Sioux, who led a resistance to U.S. government policies.

massacred General Custer and around 200 members of the Seventh Cavalry.

Control of the reservations was transferred to the Army, and the Sioux Appropriation Bill withdrew subsistence unless the Sioux relinquished their rights to the hunting grounds outside the reservation and ceded the Black Hills to the U.S. The Congressional Act (1877) required the Sioux to relinquish the Black Hills and surrounding territory; the 1889 Sioux Act opened up more land to white settlers. In 1890, a huge Sioux uprising ended when Sitting Bull, principal chief of the entire Sioux nation, was killed at Pine Ridge Reservation while being arrested for refusing orders not to attend the Ghost Dance gatherings. Two weeks later, Sioux resistance crumbled completely following the Wounded Knee Massacre by the revitalized Seventh Cavalry. It was the Year of Lost Hope not only for the Sioux, but for all Native Americans battling to retain their lands.

The twentieth century saw mixed fortunes for the indigenous population. In 1906, Charles Curtis became the first person with Native American ancestry to be elected to the Senate. The Mesa Verde National Park was created under the Federal Antiquities Act (1906) to preserve the Ancestral Pueblan site discovered in 1874. The Society of American Indians, the first national Native American political organization, was formed in 1911 and the Native American Church established in 1918. The Indian Citizenship Act (1924) granted citizenship to all Native Americans born in

Students conduct physics experiments at the Carlisle Indian School in Pennsylvania, the first federally funded off-reservation Indian boarding school (c. 1915).

the U.S. The National Congress of American Indians (NCAI) was formed in 1944 to serve the interests of tribal governments and communities. However, a 1943 survey of Indian conditions resulted in the Termination Era (1953–68), with the government aiming to eradicate the Indian tribes. State governments adopted federal responsibility and jurisdiction, tribal lands were sold to non-Indians, tribes lost official recognition, and more than a quarter of Native American children were placed with non-Indian families by the Bureau of Indian Affairs and the Child Welfare League. The 1968 Indian Civil Rights Act replaced "termination" with "self-determination" and aimed to guarantee Indians living under tribal governments the same rights as other U.S. citizens. The same year saw the foundation of the American Indian Movement (AIM), whose mission included economic independence for Native Americans, revitalization of traditional culture, protection of legal rights, autonomy over tribal areas, and the restoration of lands. AIM protests included the occupation of Alcatraz Island by Indians of All Tribes (1969–71), which brought Indian rights issues to both federal and public attention.

Subsequent measures to acknowledge Native American culture include the Indian Education Act (1972), which recognized the Indians' unique academic and cultural needs. The Indian Child Welfare Act (1978) suspended the practice of placing Native American children with non-Indian families and reaffirmed their right to remain Indian; the American Indian Religious Freedom Act was also passed that year. The Native American Languages Act (1990) recognized the unique status of the cultures and languages of Native Americans, and their history, traditions, and values are now celebrated annually in November—Native American Heritage Month.

Cliff Palace, the largest of the Anasazi Indian ruins in Mesa Verde National Park, Colorado, was constructed inside natural alcoves.

THE EXPLORERS

Painter Sebastiano del Piombo's *Portrait of a Man, Said to be Christopher Columbus* (c. 1519) depicts the New World explorer.

The early European explorers of the New World set sail with no notion that they would make such a momentous discovery. They were simply seeking a westward route to Asia, where riches such as gold and spices were to be found, the eastward land and sea routes used by earlier voyagers and merchants having become unviable as a result of Christian/Islamic conflict.

The first European explorer to reach the shores of North America was, however, on a different mission. He is believed to have been an eleventh-century Viking, Leif Erikson, who sailed off course on a return voyage to Norway from Greenland, where he had been fulfilling a commission to convert Greenland settlers to Christianity. It is thought that he established the settlement discovered in 1963 by archeologists at L'Anse aux Meadows, Newfoundland, now a UNESCO World Heritage Site.

By the time Columbus embarked on his first voyage of discovery aboard the *Santa María* on August 3, 1492, the globe had already opened up considerably as intrepid European adventurers set out on small, ill-equipped ships to engage in trade and acquire knowledge of the wider world, specifically the Far East. In the late thirteenth century, the Venetian merchant and traveler Marco Polo visited Asia, and it was his description of Cipangu (Japan) in the account of his travels—*Il Milione*—that inspired Columbus to visit that country himself. He expected to encounter nothing but open sea between Europe and Asia, so when land was sighted on October 12, he assumed he had arrived in the Indies. In fact, he had found the Bahamas. He explored further, convinced that the extensive coastline of the island he named Juana (Cuba) was Cathay (China), although the absence of great cities or towns bewildered him.

Columbus claimed the islands for Spain "by proclamation and display of the Royal Standard." He then discovered and named La Isla Española (Hispaniola, now Haiti and the Dominican Republic), and waxed lyrical about its beauty, describing it as "a marvel." On his second voyage, in 1493–96, Columbus concluded that Hispaniola had the most to offer among the islands in terms of gold and other riches. He declared it to be the biblical land of Sheba and established new settlements there, including La Isabela and Santo Tomás. He still believed Cuba to be the mainland of China, and thus the aim of his third voyage, in 1498, was to find a strait from Cuba to India. He discovered northern Venezuela, where he planted the Spanish flag on the Paria Peninsula, but not—of course—the strait. He returned one last time, in 1502, when he explored the coasts of Jamaica, Cuba, Honduras, Nicaragua, Costa Rica, and Panama, always in search of the elusive strait. He died in Spain in 1506, still believing he had reached Asia. The news of Columbus's discovery was disseminated throughout Europe via copies of his correspondence, which was translated into several languages. The only known complete copy of the illustrated Latin edition of his first report to his sponsors, Ferdinand and Isabella, is held by The New York Public Library.

In 1497, another Italian-born explorer, Giovanni Caboto—better known by his Anglicized name, John Cabot—set sail from the port of Bristol on *Matthew*, on a voyage sponsored by the English king Henry VII. He made landfall on the coast of North America on June 24 and claimed what he called "new-found-land" for England—he, too, believing he had reached Asia. He then sailed south along the coast toward Maine before returning to England. He intended to return to his landing place the following year and from there sail westward to Japan, but his second expedition disappeared without trace. Cabot's son Sebastian subsequently led an English expedition in search of a northwest passage to Asia in 1509 and a Spanish expedition to South America in 1525–28. He published a map of the world in 1544.

Meanwhile, a third Italian-born explorer and navigator, Amerigo Vespucci, had explored the coast of South America on two expeditions. He believed the first expedition, undertaken under the Spanish flag in 1499–1500, had taken him along the extreme easterly peninsula of Asia. The second expedition took place in 1501–02 under the Portuguese flag, and this exploration convinced Vespucci that the newly discovered lands were in fact separate from Asia. His accounts of the indigenous peoples were published in a number of languages and distributed across Europe, and in 1507 a German cartographer, Martin Waldseemüller, printed the first map of the New World bearing the name "America."

In 1508–09, Juan Ponce de León, who had been appointed provincial governor of eastern Hispaniola, explored Puerto Rico in search of gold and founded Caparra, the colony's oldest settlement. Encouraged by the Spanish crown, he continued his exploration of the area, and it was while he was in search of the island of Bimini and its mythical fountain of youth that he landed on the mainland of North America—although he believed it to be another island. He named the region Florida and in 1514 was granted permission to colonize both Florida and Bimini; however, he was fatally wounded during a native attack on his return journey to Florida.

In 1504, Hernán Cortés, who would become one of the most famous Spanish conquistadors, arrived on the island of Hispaniola. He took part in the conquest of Cuba in 1511, and in 1518 he set sail in command of an expedition to Mexico. He established a settlement (now Veracruz) the following year, and was then invited by Montezuma II, king of the Atzec civilization, to visit their capital, Tenochtitlán. It is thought that Montezuma's warm welcome was based on his interpretation of Cortés as the "white-skinned god arriving from the east" of Aztec prophecy; he was soon disillusioned, and in 1521 Tenochtitlán fell to Spanish forces, bringing an end to the mighty Aztec empire. Spanish colonists established a new settlement, Mexico City, which became the center of New Spain. Cortés continued to explore Central America, and in 1536 he explored the northwest region and Pacific coast of Mexico and discovered the Baja California peninsula.

Meanwhile, another Spanish conquistador, Panfilo de Narváez, had claimed the region around Tampa Bay in Florida for Spain; and in 1539 Hernando de Soto, who had assisted in the conquest of Peru, explored the southeastern region of North America (Florida, Georgia, and Alabama) and discovered the Mississippi River. The following year, Francisco Vásquez de Coronado embarked on a mission to search for the legendary Seven Golden Cities of Cíbola

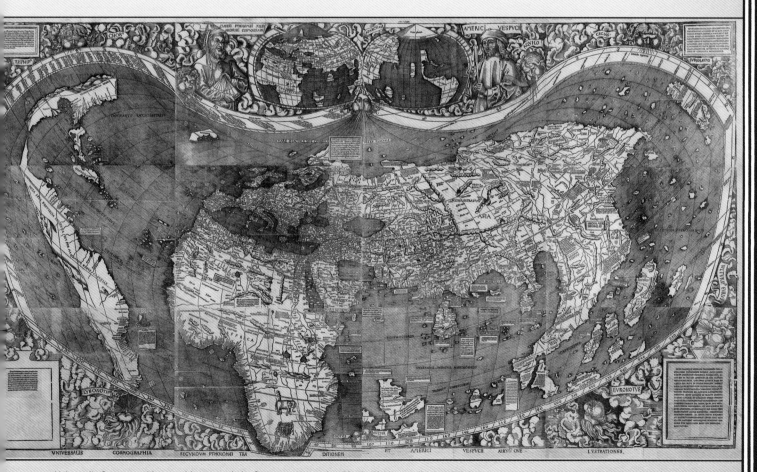

Universalis Cosmographia, a world map made by German cartographer Martin Waldseemuller in 1507, is known as the first map to use the name "America."

Painter William H. Powell's *Discovery of the Mississippi by De Soto* shows conqueror and explorer Hernando De Soto, the first European to view the Mississippi River.

reported by an earlier explorer, Álvar Núñez Cabeza de Vaca. While Coronado failed to locate the cities, his expeditionary parties discovered American Southwest landmarks including the Grand Canyon. In 1542, Juan Rodríguez Cabrillo, a Portuguese explorer in the service of Spain, sailed into San Diego Bay, becoming the first European to navigate the coast of California. At that point, California was believed to be an island—it was not until 1705 that Spanish cartographers established that it was a peninsula. The Cabrillo National

Monument, established in 1913, commemorates the explorer's achievement.

While the Spanish and Portuguese at first dominated exploration of the New World, it was by no means exclusively theirs. For example, in 1524, Giovanni da Verrazzano, an Italian navigator and explorer for France aboard the *Delfina*, explored the eastern coast of North America from Cape Fear, North Carolina. He became the first European to enter New York Harbor and the Hudson River and also discovered

year, he explored the St. Lawrence River as far as Quebec, where he established a base, and then carried on to Montréal Island. A third expedition, in 1541, was less successful and French interest in the New World temporarily waned, but Cartier's exploration established the French fur trade with the Native Americans (in Canada, the First Nations). Over a hundred years later, in 1673, a French Jesuit explorer, Jacques Marquette, accompanied the French-Canadian explorer and cartographer Louis Jolliet on an expedition to traverse the Mississippi, which they followed to the mouth of the Arkansas River. In 1682, the French explorer René-Robert Cavelier, Sieur de la Salle, consolidated French claims to the Mississippi watershed—a vast area, and the most fertile region of North America—and named it Louisiana.

In 1577, Queen Elizabeth I commissioned the English sailor and navigator Francis Drake to undertake an expedition aboard the *Golden Hind* against the Spanish colonies on the American Pacific coast. Having plundered Spanish ports on the west coast of South America, Drake continued north and sailed farther up the west coast of North America than any European to date, claiming the area around San Francisco Bay for England. Ten years later, his fellow countryman Sir Walter Raleigh explored from North Carolina to Florida, having been granted the right by Elizabeth I, the "Virgin Queen," to colonize land in America. He named the region "Virginia" in her honor.

Thus, within two hundred years of Columbus's historic voyage, European navigators had explored much of the coastline of the New World and were making their presence felt inland as they claimed territories for their native countries and challenged each other for supremacy. There was still much to discover, however—not least the elusive northwest route to Asia, which explorers only gradually pieced together. The most significant advance in terms of Asia was Vitus Bering's confirmation in 1728 that Asia and America were two separate continents. Bering's subsequent Great Nordic Expedition in 1733–43, on behalf of Russia, was the largest expedition ever organized and mapped the west coast of Alaska. The Northwest Passage was eventually identified in the mid nineteenth century but the whole route was not successfully navigated until Norwegian explorer Roald Amundsen's expedition in 1903–06.

Despite their extraordinary discoveries and contribution to global development, many New World explorers died disillusioned or disgraced, while others were murdered by natives during a voyage, or perished in storms, or simply vanished without trace.

Block Island and Narragansett Bay, Rhode Island. New York's Verrazano-Narrows Bridge is named in his honor, and the Hudson River, Bay, and Strait for the English explorer Henry Hudson, who in 1609 navigated the river as far as Albany in search of a northwest route to Asia and claimed the entire valley for his sponsors, the Dutch East India Company.

In 1534, the French sailor Jacques Cartier embarked on his first voyage to North America, during which he explored the west coast of Newfoundland, discovered Prince Edward Island, and explored the Gulf of St. Lawrence. The following

The Colonists

The arrival of the explorers in the New World was rapidly followed by colonization of the regions as they were discovered. The very first European settlement was established on Christmas Day, 1492, by Columbus himself, on the northern coast of Hispaniola. It consisted of a small fortress built with materials from the wreckage of his ship, *Santa María*, which had run aground. Columbus named the settlement La Navidad ("the Nativity"). When he returned the following year, he found that natives had massacred the men he had left to guard the settlement. It was the first of countless conflicts between natives and Europeans.

The Voyage of the Mayflower shows the ship that brought the first pilgrims to New England around 1620.

On his second voyage, Columbus was accompanied by friars tasked with Christianizing the natives, as well as ships bearing colonists and investors. By 1508, around 10,000 Spanish colonists had settled in the West Indies. The oldest continuously occupied European settlement in the mainland United States is the city of Saint Augustine in northeastern Florida, founded in 1565. It was the northernmost outpost of the Spanish colonial empire, constructed to protect Spanish lands from an increasing threat from France.

Further north, British colonization of America began with the establishment of a settlement on Roanoke Island, North Carolina, sponsored by the explorer Sir Walter Raleigh. A research party arrived on the island in 1584 on an exploratory mission, followed by a second the following year; the first group reported great potential for a settlement, but the second clashed with the natives and returned to England. In 1587, a third group arrived, including families, who would become both the first English-speaking settlers in America and the source of an enduring mystery. That year, the colonist Eleanor Dare gave birth to Virginia, the first English child born in America and the granddaughter of John White, the colony's governor. White sailed back to England for supplies and when he returned in 1590, having been delayed, he found no sign of either the colony or its inhabitants, except for the word "Croatoan" (a nearby island) carved on a palisade. The fate of the colonists remains a matter of speculation, although research continues. Since 1937, the Lost Colony of Roanoke has been commemorated annually in Manteo through a symphonic drama, and Dare County is named in honor of Virginia Dare.

The first permanent English settlement—Jamestown, Virginia—was funded by the joint-stock Virginia Company of London and founded on the banks of the James River on May 14, 1607. Three ships—*Susan Constant*, *Godspeed*, and *Discovery*—carried the first colonists, who were charged with settling land between the 34th and 41st Parallel, near Chesapeake Bay. There were men and boys only, although the Virginia Company later recruited "young, handsome and honestly educated maydes" as prospective brides for the settlers. The settlers erected a three-sided fort and set about establishing industries, their aim to generate profits for the company stockholders. Survival was challenging, however, and many of the settlers perished. The first two leaders proved ineffectual but the third, Captain John Smith, provided brief but strong leadership and the colony began to flourish. In 1608–09, around 600 new colonists set sail for Virginia, many of whom did not survive the "Starving Time" of the harsh winter of 1609–10; recent evidence suggests that the settlers resorted to cannibalism in their desperation.

Their difficulties were further compounded by a deteriorating relationship with the powerful native Powhatan confederacy, whose estimated population in eastern Virginia was around 21,000 when the settlers arrived. There were also financial problems, which were only resolved when John Rolfe, who had arrived in 1610 with a new influx of colonists, harvested and exported the first successful tobacco crop. Rolfe is also remembered in the legend of Pocahontas, the daughter of Chief Powhatan, whom Captain Samuel Argall took hostage in 1613 and Rolfe married the following year.

The marriage brought an end to the First Anglo-Powhatan War and resulted in a truce with the tribe; this lasted long enough for the settlers to develop their colony and expand the settlement far beyond Jamestown, establishing lucrative tobacco plantations along the James River. There were further problems, however. By 1621 the Virginia Company was severely in debt, and in 1622 the Powhatans massacred nearly a quarter of the settlers in a new attack. In 1624 James I, after whom the colony was named, assumed control; the Virginia Assembly received royal approval in 1627.

Meanwhile, on November 9, 1620, a ship called the *Mayflower* had reached the shores of Cape Cod, carrying the thirty-five English colonists whom the orator Daniel Webster would, at the bicentennial celebration of their arrival, call the Pilgrim Fathers. The Pilgrims were Separatists, a Puritan sect who had fled from Scrooby in Nottinghamshire to seek freedom from religious persecution in Holland, where they settled in Leiden in 1609. However, low wages and the threat of war with Spain, a staunchly Catholic country, prompted them to relocate to the New World, and they sailed from Plymouth, Devon on September 6, 1620. Their fellow passengers onboard the *Mayflower* were representatives of the London company of merchant adventurers who financed the expedition. These included a cooper, John Alden, traditionally the first colonist to set foot on Plymouth Rock, although early accounts make no mention of this, and a soldier, Miles Standish. According to folklore, Standish was widowed soon after their arrival in America, and asked Alden to propose on his behalf to Priscilla Mullins, another *Mayflower* passenger. Priscilla, however, suggested that John should speak "for himself"—he did, and John and Priscilla were married

instead. Their story was immortalized in Henry Wadsworth Longfellow's narrative poem about the early days of the colony, *The Courtship of Miles Standish.*

On November 11, before disembarking, the head of every family onboard the ship signed the "Mayflower Compact," the first written framework of government in the U.S. The Compact created a Civil Body Politic to enact "just and equal Laws, Ordinances, Acts, Constitution and Offices." It was drawn up to prevent dissent between the Separatist and non-Separatist colonists, and was necessary because, owing to storms and a near shipwreck, the colonists had landed outside the jurisdiction of the First Pierce Patent, the charter that granted the merchant adventurers permission to establish a new settlement in the Virginia Territory. The Second Pierce Patent, confirming the Pilgrims' settlement and governance of Plymouth, was granted by the Council for New England in 1621. A third patent, the Bradford Patent, was granted in 1630. This enabled the Pilgrims to buy out the company of merchant adventurers, whose shareholders were entitled under the original contract to a share of all the assets accrued in the colony after a period of seven years. The original Mayflower Compact has been lost, but the exact wording was published in London in 1622 in an account of the colony's establishment. The first signatory on the Compact and the colony's first governor was the Separatist John Carver, who died within six months of their arrival; he was succeeded by William Bradford, whose handwritten history *Of Plymouth Plantation* also includes the text of the Compact.

As with the Jamestown settlers, the first winter in the Plymouth colony was unforgiving and half the settlers perished, from disease and harsh conditions; despite this, none of

The March of Miles Standish (c. 1873) depicts the English military officer who was elected as the first officer of the Plymouth Colony militia.

the survivors opted to return to England when the Mayflower sailed back. Their fortunes changed when Samoset, a chief of the native Abenaki people, walked into the settlement on March 16 and welcomed the colonists in broken English. He provided the colonists with useful information about the region and, critically, arranged an introduction to Massasoit, great sachem (chief) of the neighboring Wampanoag people, who was keen to forge an alliance with the colonists against more powerful tribes. Edward Winslow was delegated to liaise with Massasoit, with whom he developed a firm friendship. Massasoit's emissary Tisquantum ("Squanto") served as guide and interpreter, and on April 1, 1621, the colonists and Wampanoag agreed an alliance of mutual support.

Over the summer of 1621, the colony began to thrive. Food was plentiful and the surviving members were in good health. In the fall, Massasoit and other members of the Wampanoag joined the colonists for their harvest festival, the event known as the First Thanksgiving in Plymouth. The first recorded religious Thanksgiving was held in 1623 and over time the custom was established of an annual Thanksgiving, the date being proclaimed by individual governors. In the mid 1800s, the writer and magazine editor Sarah Josepha Hale campaigned for a national annual Thanksgiving holiday, which Lincoln declared in 1863.

In 1691 the Plymouth colony was merged, under a royal charter issued by William III, with the Massachusetts Bay Colony. The Boston colony was settled in 1630 by a group of English Puritan refugees under Governor John Winthrop. The colony's original charter, obtained by the Massachusetts Bay Company, differed from earlier charters in that it was administered in America, rather than from England. The colony quickly became successful and Boston was the largest town in British North America until the mid 1700s, when Philadelphia, capital of the Commonwealth of Pennsylvania established in 1681 by the Quaker leader William Penn, surpassed Boston in both size and importance. Also growing in importance was the strategically located city of New Amsterdam, established in 1626 by Peter Minuit, Director General of the Dutch West India Company. Situated on Manhattan, which Minuit

purchased from its native population for 60 guilders' worth of trade goods, it was the capital of America's only Dutch colony, New Netherland. When Peter Stuyvesant was appointed Director General of the colony in 1645, one of his first tasks on

This statue of Massasoit honors the Great Sachem of the Wampanoags, who helped form an alliance between the Pilgrims and the Wampanoags in Massachusetts.

Robert Walter Weir's painting *Embarkation of the Pilgrims* (1857) depicts a group of Pilgrims on the deck of a ship before their 1620 voyage from Holland to the New World.

arrival was to establish a municipal government for the city. Although the British seized control of New Netherland in 1664, renaming its capital New York for Charles II's brother, James, Duke of York, the Dutch left a legacy of a cosmopolitan city at the heart of a colony made prosperous by trade. Martin van Buren, the eighth U.S. president, was descended from the Dutch settlers.

A French Jesuit missionary, Father Jacques Marquette, founded Sault Ste. Marie, Michigan's first European settlement, in 1668, followed by a second, St. Ignace, in 1671, before joining Louis Jolliet on his exploration of the interior of North America that would lead to France claiming the Mississippi watershed. The fight between Britain and France for supremacy on the North American continent began in 1689 with the outbreak of King William's War, the first of four wars that concluded with France ceding its territory east of the Mississippi to Britain under the 1763 Treaty of Paris, while Spain acquired Louisiana.

THE WAR OF INDEPENDENCE

The French and Indian War (1754–63) left Britain with huge territorial gains in North America—and an equally huge national debt. In addition, Native Americans inhabiting formerly French colonial territories objected to the new British rule and staged a rebellion led by Pontiac, an Ottawa chief. As a result, the British Prime Minister, Lord Bute, decided to maintain a standing army in North America, which also required funding.

In an attempt to raise revenue through the colonies so that they would effectively pay for their own protection, Bute's successor, Lord Grenville, introduced two regulatory acts in 1764. The American Revenue Act—or, more commonly, the Sugar Act—stemmed from a series of Navigation Acts passed between 1660 and 1696, which required all colonial trade to be carried out on English ships. The Sugar Act provided for customs enforcement on imports of foreign molasses, as well as numerous other commodities, and curbed smuggling of molasses from the French West Indies—a cheaper option than the British product. This led in turn to a decline in the colonies' significant rum industry and a major disruption in colonial exports of other goods. Grenville's Currency Act assumed control of the previously unregulated colonial currency system. In 1690, the Massachusetts Bay Colony had introduced paper money in response to a shortage of coinage which, along with the Native American *wampum* (shell beads), was the principal form of currency at the time. The system, essentially in the form of bills of credit, was quickly adopted by other colonies, but it was haphazard, with no common standard value. The Currency Act abolished the use of colonial bills and prohibited both the issue of new bills and the reissue of existing ones. Again, this adversely affected colonial trade.

Dissent over the two acts was compounded the following year by the Stamp Act, which required all legal documents, licenses, commercial contracts, newspapers, pamphlets, and playing cards to carry a tax stamp. The Act had the effect of uniting the thirteen colonies against the British government. The colonists issued petitions denying Parliament's authority

The Latin text on the scroll of this Massachusetts Regimental Drum from the Revolutionary War period says, "It's sweet and distinguished to die for one's country."

to tax the colonies—since they had no direct representation in Parliament, their battle cry became "No taxation without representation"—and imposed a boycott on British goods. Parliament repealed the Act, bringing a short-lived peace that ended with the four Townshend Acts (1767), an attempt to exert authority over the colonies through the imposition of new taxes and the suspension of self-government. The Acts were met with resistance, expressed both verbally and physically, and in 1770 a skirmish in Boston ended with the murder of five colonists by British troops. The Acts were repealed, coincidentally on the same day as the Boston Massacre—but the revenue duties on tea remained in place.

In 1773, the British Tea Act granted the East India Company a monopoly on the tax-free transport of tea in order to prevent the company's bankruptcy. The provisions of the Act were so beneficial to the East India Company that colonial tea traders were unable to compete. Resistance to the Act led to the Boston Tea Party, the turning point in colonial history. On November 29, 1773, a handbill was posted all over Boston announcing the imminent arrival of the East India Company ship *Dartmouth*, bearing a consignment of tea. The Massachusetts Bay colonists resolved to prevent the tea being landed, and on December 16 a group of 116 men, some disguised as Indians, boarded the *Dartmouth* and two other ships, the *Eleanor* and *Beaver*, moored at Griffin's Wharf. Watched by more than 5,000 silent onlookers, the men emptied 342 chests containing a total of 45 tons of tea into Boston Harbor.

The British response was to take punitive measures in the form of what became known as the Coercive or Intolerable Acts (1774). The Boston Port Bill closed the port pending compensation for the destroyed tea. The Massachusetts Government Act abrogated the colony's 1691 charter and placed it under military control with General Thomas Gage as governor. The Administration of Justice Act allowed for British officials charged with capital offenses during law enforcement in a colony to be tried

The BLOODY MASSACRE perpetuated in King-Street BOSTON on March 5th 1770 by a party of the 29th REGT.

Unhappy Boston! see thy Sons deplore,
Thy hallow'd Walks besmear'd with guiltless Gore:
While faithless P——n and his savage Bands,
With murd'rous Rancour stretch their bloody Hands;
Like fierce Barbarians grinning o'er their Prey,
Approve the Carnage, and enjoy the Day.

If scalding drops from Rage from Anguish Wrung
If speechless Sorrows lab'ring for a Tongue,
Or if a weeping World can ought appease
The plaintive Ghosts of Victims such as these:
The Patriot's copious Tears for each are shed,
A glorious Tribute which embalms the Dead.

But know, Fate summons to that awful Goal.
Where Justice strips the Murd'rer of his Soul:
Should venal C——ts the scandal of the Land,
Snatch the relentless Villain from her Hand,
Keen Execrations on this Plate inscrib'd,
Shall reach a Judge who never can be brib'd.

Engrav'd Printed & Sold by Paul Revere Boston

The unhappy Sufferers were Messrs. Saml. Gray, Saml. Maverick, Jams. Caldwell, Crispus Attucks & Patk. Carr
Killed. Six wounded: two of them (Christr. Monk & John Clark) Mortally
Published in 1770 by Paul Revere Boston

This artwork depicts the Boston Massacre on March 5, 1770, when seven British soldiers opened fire into a crowd of Boston civilians at the behest of their officer.

in England or a different colony. The fourth Act included arrangements for housing British troops in occupied American dwellings.

On September 5, 1774, the First Continental Congress convened in Philadelphia, with Peyton Randolph of Virginia as president and Charles Thomson of Pennsylvania as secretary, to discuss an appropriate response to the Intolerable Acts. The delegates—56 in all—also included George Washington, Patrick Henry, John and Samuel Adams, John Jay, and John Dickinson. Every colony except Georgia was represented and each was given one vote, regardless of size. On October 14, the delegates adopted the Declaration

John Trumbull's *General George Washington Before the Battle of Trenton* (c. 1792) depicts a decisive moment of Washington's leadership that led to a major turning point in the Revolutionary War.

and Resolves on Colonial Rights of the First Continental Congress. The resolutions, drafted by Major John Sullivan, included a declaration of the right to life, liberty, and property and listed the Acts of Parliament that infringed and violated the rights of the colonists, noting that their repeal was "essentially necessary in order to restore harmony between Great Britain and the American colonies." The delegates petitioned George III for a redress of grievances, resolved unanimously to boycott British goods with effect from December 1, and agreed to convene a second meeting of Congress on May 10, 1775.

Meanwhile, Governor Gage advised the British government that if the Intolerable Acts were not suspended, he would require reinforcements in order to crush the rebellion he believed was imminent. The British government disagreed, convinced that only further punitive measures would resolve the problem. On February 1, 1775, John Hancock and Joseph Warren commenced defensive preparations for a state of war at a provincial congress held in Cambridge, Massachusetts; later that month the British government declared Massachusetts to be in a state of rebellion. On March 23, Patrick Henry spoke out against British rule, famously declaring, ". . . I know not what course others may take; but as for me, give me liberty or give me death!"

The New England Restraining Act, passed on March 30, required New England colonies to trade exclusively with England. General Gage was then ordered to enforce the Coercive Acts and use all necessary force to suppress rebellion, and on April 18 he dispatched 700 soldiers to Concord to destroy the colonists' weapons depot. The following day, with peaceful negotiation no longer even a possibility, the Revolutionary War began with a "shot heard around the world." The initial battles at Concord and Lexington ended badly for the colonists, leaving ten dead, but within days thousands of volunteers had been mobilized and British-held Boston was under siege. On May 10, American forces captured Fort Ticonderoga in New York and removed military equipment to Boston, while the Second Continental Congress convened as planned and declared the colonies in a state of defense. George Washington was appointed general and commander-in-chief of the new Continental Army; he proved to be an outstanding military strategist.

In June 1775, the first major battle of the war, at Bunker Hill, Boston, ended with significant losses on both sides. Congress then issued a Declaration on the Causes and Necessity of Taking Up Arms, stating that the Americans were "resolved to die free men rather than live as slaves." In January 1776, the local assembly of New Hampshire declared its independence from Britain and enacted the first American constitution. A few days later, Thomas Paine published a pamphlet entitled "Common Sense," advocating independence for the American colonies and stating: "We have it in our power to begin the world anew." These two events provided the inspiration the other colonies needed, and in May 1776 Congress authorized all colonies to establish their own provincial or state governments. A committee consisting of Thomas Jefferson, Benjamin Franklin, John Adams, Roger Livingston, and Roger Sherman then met to draft a declaration of independence, of which Jefferson was the principal author. On July 2, twelve of the colonies—Connecticut, Delaware, Georgia, Maryland, Massachusetts, New Hampshire, New Jersey, North Carolina, Pennsylvania, Rhode Island, South Carolina, and Virginia—voted in support of independence (New York abstained). Two days later, Congress adopted the Declaration of Independence, and the document was signed on August 2.

The American troops suffered several defeats through the fall of 1776, leading Thomas Paine to comment that "Tyranny, like Hell, is not easily conquered" but that ". . . the harder the conflict, the more glorious the triumph." On October 7, 1777, the Battle of Saratoga resulted in the first major victory for the Americans. The British forces under General Burgoyne surrendered and returned to England. On November 15, Congress adopted the Articles of Confederation, which established the functions of the national government of the new United States of America; by 1781, they had been ratified by all thirteen states.

After the victory at Saratoga, France formally acknowledged the United States as an independent nation. France had become an ally of the revolutionaries early on in the war, supplying arms and munitions, and one of Washington's most trusted aides was a young French aristocrat, Marquis de Lafayette. On February 6, 1778, American and French representatives signed a Treaty of Amity and Commerce and a Treaty of Alliance. France now entered the war.

Meanwhile, Washington had spent the winter with his troops at Valley Forge, Pennsylvania, where he worked tirelessly to improve services to the soldiers. This boost to their morale, together with rigorous training by an ex-Prussian Army General Staff member, Baron Friedrich von Stuben, imbued the soldiers with new determination. Despite this, the worst American defeat of the war took place in May 1780, when the siege of Charleston culminated in surrender to the British of forces numbering around 5,000. Morale was again low and mutiny rife among the troops, but the end of military operations was in sight. It came on October 19, 1781, with the surrender of 9,000 British following the siege of Yorktown. The Treaty of Paris (1783) formally ended the war and Britain acknowledged her former colonies to be "free, sovereign, and independent States." Congress ratified the treaty on January 14, 1784.

As the new nation began to find its feet, the need for a strong federal government became clear. A Constitutional Convention was held in 1787 to amend the 1777 Articles of Confederation and on March 4, 1789, they were replaced by the present United States Constitution. The content of the Bill of Rights was strongly influenced by that of the English Magna Carta (Great Charter of Liberties), signed in 1215 and enshrined in statute law in 1297, which stated that "No free man shall be arrested, imprisoned, dispossessed, outlawed, exiled or in any way victimized, or attacked except by the lawful judgement of his peers or by the law of the land."

John Trumbull's painting *Declaration of Independence* shows five of the Founding Fathers presenting the Declaration to Congress.

THE INDUSTRIAL REVOLUTION

The Industrial Revolution that changed the face of America began in Britain in the early 1700s, when coal replaced wood as a source of energy. Coal was plentiful but the risk of flooding made the deeper seams difficult to access; however, in 1712, Thomas Newcomen, a blacksmith, invented the atmospheric steam engine, which enabled water to be pumped from hundreds of feet below ground. The design of Newcomen's machine was subsequently improved and patented in 1769 by James Watt, whose company Boulton & Watt produced steam engines tailored for a range of manufacturing processes, including cotton and iron—both of which would influence economic growth in the new United States.

Boys overlook the Homestead steel plant in Pittsburgh in 1903.

Cotton manufacturing became a major industry in the north of England, facilitated by several inventions—John Kay's flying shuttle (1733), James Hargreaves's spinning jenny (1764), (a different) John's Kay's spinning frame (1767) and Arkwright's water frame (1769). The new machines enabled a vastly increased level of productivity, in turn requiring a greater import of the raw material. Green-seed cotton was widely available in the American South, but cleaning the seed and extracting the fiber was a laborious process. However, in 1794, Eli Whitney patented one of the key inventions of the Industrial Revolution, a "cotton gin" (cotton engine) that mechanized the process, transforming cotton production into a highly profitable business.

The first American cotton mill was established in 1790 at Pawtucket, Rhode Island, by Samuel Slater, who completed an apprenticeship as a cotton spinner in England before emigrating to America. In 1794, John and Arthur Schofield, also from England, established America's first woolen mill. In 1813, the Boston Manufacturing Company was formed, America's first textile factory with all the technology to undertake the whole process of cotton manufacture. By the 1860s there were more than 1,200 cotton factories and 1,500 woolen factories in the U.S. Other factory industries also burgeoned rapidly; an important factor was the introduction of the "corporation," which encouraged investment by limiting investor liability for business debts to the extent of their investment.

Early industrial growth was driven by Alexander Hamilton, the new nation's first Secretary of the Treasury (1789–95), who recognized the need for a secure U.S. economy to maximize the commercial potential of the output of the new technologies. An official federal monetary system based on the Spanish dollar was agreed in 1785, the First Bank of the United States was chartered in 1791, and the Coinage Act (1792) created the U.S. mint. The list of coinage specified in the Act ranged from the gold eagle, half eagle and quarter eagle (ten, five, and two-and-a-half dollars) to silver dollars, half dollars, quarter dollars, "dismes" (dimes) and half dimes, and lastly the copper cent and half cent. The coins would bear the words "United States of America" and "an impression emblematic of liberty, with an inscription of the word Liberty, and the year of the coinage." The first American coin, a half dime, was struck in July 1792.

The invention of steam power also spawned new innovations in transportation, which in turn expedited the progress of the Industrial Revolution. On August 26, 1791, James Rumsey, John Fitch, and John Stevens were all granted patents for variations on the application of steam (the U.S. Patent Act was passed in 1790). Rumsey's was for "application of steam to propel boats or vessels," Fitch's for "steam engine applied to navigation," and Stevens's for "applying the force of steam." The first viable commercial steamboat was, however, Robert Fulton's *Clermont*, launched in August 1807. In 1809, Stevens's boat *Phoenix* became the first steamship to navigate ocean waters, and in 1811 he introduced the world's first steam-ferry service.

Eli Whitney's patent for the cotton gin on March 14, 1794.

In 1825, the English engineer George Stephenson launched another invention inspired by Newcomen's atmospheric engine—a steam locomotive that traveled at 15 miles per hour. The feasibility of steam locomotion was also being explored in America by John Stevens, who built an experimental locomotive in 1825 and is considered the father of the American railroad system. In 1827, the Baltimore and Ohio Railroad was granted the first U.S. railway charter for commercial transport of passengers and freight. The first stretch of track was just 13 miles long, but by 1850, 9,021 miles had been laid. In 1869, the Central Pacific and Union Pacific Lines were joined to create the first transcontinental railroad, and by the end of the century there were 166,073 miles of laid track. The construction of the railroad was a major factor in the cattle boom, which lasted for around 20 years before coming to an end in the mid 1880s. The drives to meet the railroad, where the cattle could now be conveniently transported either live or butchered and stored in refrigerated cars, are one of the iconic images of the period—in the 1960s, the TV show *Rawhide*, about the challenges faced by the "cowboys," ran for 217 episodes.

From the early 1830s, development began of sophisticated systems of communication over distances. In 1831, Joseph Henry invented the first electric telegraph. In 1836, Samuel F. B. Morse devised a method of communicating via electrical telegraphy by representing letters, numerals and punctuation with a series of dots, dashes, and spaces—the

Right: Thomas Alva Edison in his laboratory.

Below: Built by Phineas Davis, the "Atlantic" locomotive—shown here pulling two double-decked Imlay coaches—went into operation on the Baltimore and Ohio Railroad in the summer of 1832. It was the first train to enter Washington, D.C.

basis of the International Morse Code adopted in 1851—and in 1843 he patented the long-distance electric telegraph line. The following year, he transmitted the telegraph message "What hath God wrought?" from Washington to Baltimore. In 1846, Royal Earl House patented an alpha-numerical telegraph, able to print 50 words a minute. He later developed an electro-phonetic receiver for use in telegraphy, an early version of the electric telephone patented in 1876 by the Scottish inventor Alexander Graham Bell. In 1891, Almon Strowger patented the automatic telephone switch, which eliminated the need for an operator. In 1906, Lee de Forest invented the triode vacuum tube and in 1913 Edwin Armstrong developed a regenerative circuit, both for amplifying radio signals. Armstrong also developed a superheterodyne circuit for radio, and in 1933 invented the frequency-modulated (FM) radio.

One of Edison's earliest light bulbs that has survived.

In 1856, the English inventor and engineer Henry Bessemer developed a process for manufacturing steel inexpensively; his process was superseded in 1867 by the more efficient open-hearth process furnace, which became widely used and enabled the production of mild steel for the manufacture of construction materials. From the early 1870s, Andrew Carnegie, one of America's new captains of industry, revolutionized steel production in the U.S.A. and in 1892 he founded the Carnegie Steel Company. In 1901 he sold the company for $480 million to the banker J. P. Morgan, who combined the company with two other steel companies to form the United States Steel Corporation, America's first billion-dollar corporation.

Flexible Bessemer steel beams were used in the construction of tall buildings, a concept championed by George A. Fuller, whose company built the Tacoma Building in Chicago, one of the first steel-framed skyscrapers, in 1889. However, an earlier Chicago building—the Home Insurance Building, erected in 1884 from cast and wrought iron with some structural steel—is credited as the first skyscraper. Other innovations also contributed to the viability of skyscrapers, such as Elisha Otis's safety elevator, equipped with a device to prevent the elevator falling in the event of a cable breakage, and Thomas Edison's

light bulb. Edison patented the light bulb and founded the Edison Illuminating Company, later the General Electric Corporation, in 1880.

The second half of the nineteenth century also saw the rise of the oil industry. John D. Rockefeller opened his first refinery in 1863 and in 1870 he co-founded the Standard Oil Company. In 1882, he organized the Standard Oil Trust, which served as a model for monopolies; however, objections to this practice led to the Sherman Antitrust Act (1890), which dissolved the Standard Oil Company in 1911. In 1901, another industrialist and financier, Andrew Mellon, co-founded Gulf Oil; he also co-founded the Pittsburgh Reduction Company (later Alcoa) and Union Steel.

With the transition of power from manual to mechanical in industry, inventors began to explore ways to leave behind the horse when it came to individual modes of transport. In the 1830s, a Scottish inventor, Robert Anderson, designed an electric "horseless" carriage; however, in 1885 a German mechanical engineer, Karl Benz, built the world's first gasoline-powered automobile with an internal-combustion engine, setting the scene for a new global industry. In 1893, brothers Charles and Frank Duryea set up America's first car manufacturing company. Ransom E. Olds founded Olds Motor Works in Lansing, Michigan, in 1897 and in 1901 the Oldsmobile Curved Dash became the first mass-produced car. The first New York Automobile Show was held in 1900. Meanwhile, Henry Ford—at that time an

Automobile manufacturer Henry Ford takes the first "Ford" automobile, the "Quadricycle" (developed in 1892), out for a spin in 1896.

engineer with the Edison Illuminating Company—had built his first automobile, the "Quadricycle." He founded the Ford Motor Company in Detroit in 1903 and opened the first Ford dealership the same year in San Francisco, expanding into Canada in 1904 and Europe in 1908. The famous Ford Model T was launched in 1908 and produced until 1930, when it was replaced with the Model A. Ford instigated many of the innovations in automobile manufacture, most significantly the world's first moving automobile assembly line, launched in 1913. In 1918, the company opened its Rouge River "super factory" in Dearborn, Michigan, which is today being revitalized as a model of sustainable manufacturing.

The Ford company was also involved in the development of the aircraft industry. Experiments in flight had been underway for almost a hundred years before Orville and Wilbur Wright made the first successful sustained flight, on December 17, 1903, in their aircraft *Flyer I*. In 1907, the Wrights opened negotiations to supply a craft for the U.S. Army's newly formed Aeuronautical Division, which took delivery of its first military aircraft in 1909 for the purposes

of training and aerial reconnaisance. In 1925, Ford produced its Tri Motor aircraft, used in both military and civil aviation. Between 1925 and 1931, Ford sponsored National Air Tours to promote the reliability and safety of commercial aviation. Meanwhile, in 1927, Charles Lindbergh, a graduate of the Army's flight-training school, had made the first solo nonstop flight across the Atlantic in the *Spirit of St. Louis*.

The United States showcased its industrial and manufacturing achievements at expositions including the Centennial International Exhibition of 1876, the World's Columbian Exposition, held in Chicago in 1893 to celebrate the 400th anniversary of Columbus's landing in America, and the Century of Progress International Exposition held in Chicago in 1933–34.

The Wright brothers' first successful flight of the Wright Flyer on December 17, 1903. Orville piloted the plane while Wilbur ran alongside at Kill Devil Hills, near Kitty Hawk, North Carolina.

WESTWARD EXPANSION

This is the last page of the Treaty of Paris, which was signed on September 3, 1783, and ended the Revolutionary War.

Before the Treaty of Paris (1763) that concluded the French and Indian War, British settlers in North America were effectively restricted to colonizing land along the east coast. In theory, once Britain acquired the territory east of the Mississippi under the treaty, the colonists were free to start expanding beyond the western frontier; they were thwarted, however, by the Royal Proclamation of 1763, which placed the Native Americans under the protection of King George III and prohibited occupation of their lands by the colonists. He established the Proclamation Line, a boundary punctuated by military outposts, which ran from the Atlantic coast at Quebec to the border of West Florida (both now British colonies under the Proclamation). The colonists' frustration at being once again hemmed in was a factor in the lead-up to the War of Independence.

The provisions of the Quebec Act (1774) imposed further restrictions on the colonists' ambitions for expansion, as it extended Quebec's boundary westward and southward to the confluence of the Iowa and Mississippi rivers (in present-day Illinois) and placed the territory between the rivers under the governor of Quebec. Thus, even after independence, the settlers were held back.

However, from the late 1780s, settlers began expanding south-westward into the Ohio and Tennessee river valleys. For

Native American Sacagawea was an interpreter and guide to Lewis and Clark, as they explored the western United States. This statue in Bismarck, North Dakota, commemorates her important role in American history.

the purposes of trade, colonists west of the Appalachians relied on free access to the Mississippi, and in particular the port of New Orleans. The 1763 Treaty of Paris had ceded Louisiana territory to the west of the Mississippi to Spain, at that time an ally of the British; however, Spain did not develop the territory and in 1802 retroceded it to the French, with whom the Spanish were now allied. New Orleans was promptly closed to American shipping, and in 1803 President Jefferson sent James Monroe to Paris to nego-tiate purchase of the port or at least to secure U.S. access to the Mississippi and New Orleans; however, when Monroe arrived in Paris, he learned that France was offering to sell the entire Louisiana territory to the United States. Purchase of approximately 827,000 square miles of territory was completed on December 30, 1803, for a sum of $15 million, nearly doubling the size of the existing United States.

The following year, a "corps of discovery" led by two Army officers, Meriwether Lewis and William Clark, set out from Camp Wood, Illinois, to explore the Louisiana territory, where Jefferson wished to establish contact and, ultimately, trade with the Native Americans. The expedi-tion's brief was to locate a direct water route to the Pacific Ocean and also to identify and record the natural resources of the west, for which Lewis was tutored by a team of scientists. The Lewis and Clark expedition set off along the Missouri River on May 14. The first of many encounters with the native popu-lation took place on August 3 and in November the party hired Toussaint Charbonneau, a French-Canadian

In *Lewis and Clark on the Lower Columbia*, painter Charles Marion Russell depicts the intrepid explorers on the largest river of America's Pacific Northwest.

trapper, to act as interpreter and guide. Charbonneau was accompanied by his wife, Sacagawea, a Shoshone Indian who proved invaluable to the expedition. When the party reached the Missouri headwaters (now a State Park), Sacagawea negotiated with her brother, a Shoshone chief, to provide horses for the journey over the Rocky Mountains. The expedition sighted the Pacific Ocean on November 7, 1805; they began their homeward journey on March 23, 1806, arriving in St. Louis on September 23. An immediate outcome of the expedition was the establishment of the fur trade in the Rocky Mountains, which lasted until the late 1830s when the fashion for beaver hats finally died out after many centuries.

Between 1812 and 1815, the Americans fought what was effectively their second war of independence, this time against Canadian colonists and native nations as well as the British. The 1812 War began over violations of U.S. maritime rights during the ongoing conflict between Britain and France and escalated rapidly with the cessation of the Napoleonic Wars in April 1814. The Americans were confident at the outset of the war, and Thomas Jefferson even expressed the view that "the acquisition of Canada . . . will be a mere matter of marching, and will give us the experience for . . . the final expulsion of England from the American continent." However, once Britain engaged fully in the conflict, the Americans suffered a series of defeats, and on August 24, 1814, were outraged when British troops marched into Washington, D.C., established in 1790 as the seat of federal government, and set fire to the newly constructed Capitol Building and White House. On September 13, 1814, British warships began a bombardment of Fort McHenry, which protected the important seaport of Baltimore, Maryland. The U.S. troops stood their ground under the fort's commander, Lieutenant Colonel George Armistead; they fired back and the British withdrew. Baltimore was the turning point, and the war ended with the Treaty of Ghent on December 24, 1814. Critically, the British surrendered their territory in the Northwest to the U.S. and severed ties with the Native Americans, allowing future American expansion.

The success of the Lewis and Clark expedition and the outcome of the 1812 War led to a rush of westward expansion from the mid 1820s. A major factor enabling this was the construction of the 363-mile-long Erie Canal, begun in 1817 and completed in 1825, which connected Albany on the Hudson River with Buffalo on Lake Erie, opening up the land to the west of the Appalachians. It also greatly reduced the cost of shipping freight and consequently made New York the most important commercial city in the U.S. The rise of steamboat transportation also facilitated westward expansion, as did the Webster–Ashburton Treaty (1842) between the U.S. and Britain, which redefined the position of the U.S.–Canada border in the Great Lakes region in favor of the U.S.

The Great Migration westward began in earnest in the 1840s and lasted for about 40 years, spurred by the publication in 1845 of an article by John L. O'Sullivan, editor of the *United States Magazine and Democratic Review*, in which he expressed the belief that it was "our [Anglo-Americans'] manifest destiny to overspread the continent allotted by Providence for the free development of our yearly multiplying millions."

The majority of pioneers traveled overland on the 2,000-mile-long Oregon Trail. In 1818, an agreement between Britain and the U.S. had established the western border between the U.S. and Canada along the 49th Parallel from Lake of the Woods in the east to the Rocky Mountains in the west. They also agreed a joint occupation of Oregon territory, which lasted until the establishment of the trail. James K. Polk proposed renegotiating the border to bring part of Vancouver and Alberta into the U.S., famously declaring in his 1846 presidential campaign "Fifty-four forty or fight!" To avoid yet another Anglo-American war, however, the Oregon Treaty (1846) maintained the borderline on the 49th Parallel but extended it to the Strait of Georgia.

The Oregon Trail started in Independence in western Missouri and followed a route across the Great Plains, passing through Nebraska, Wyoming, Idaho, and finally reaching the 547-mile stretch through Oregon, where the trail ended in the fertile Willamette Valley. The first major wagon train, bearing around a thousand pioneers, set off from Independence on May 22, 1843. The covered wagons were known as "prairie schooners," a smaller and lighter version of the Conestoga wagons used for hauling freight before the Industrial Revolution introduced easier methods. The hardships of wagon train migration were eventually relieved by the construction of the transcontinental railway, which linked Omaha, Nebraska, in the east with Sacramento, California, in the west.

On January 24, 1848, gold was discovered in the tailrace of a newly constructed sawmill in California. A few days later, territory from Texas to Oregon, including California, was ceded to the U.S. under the Treaty of Guadelupe Hidalgo between the U.S. and Mexico, which ended the

Painter Alfred Jacob Miller's *Breaking up Camp at Sunrise* (c. 1858–60) depicts life along the Oregon Trail.

Daniel Freeman, shown here holding a gun and with a hatchet tucked into his belt, was the "first homesteader," who settled in Beatrice, Nebraska, in 1863.

in 1876–77 and in the Klondike River in Canada's Yukon region, which attracted American prospectors and inspired Jack London's novels *The Call of the Wild* and *White Fang*.

A major inducement to potential emigrants was the passage of the Homestead Act (1862), which entitled anyone over the age of 21, either a citizen or person wishing to gain citizenship, to acquire 160 acres of land in the public domain. The conditions of ownership were a filing fee of $18 and settlement of the land for a minimum of five years, during which time the homesteader was required to build a home and establish a successful farm. A total of 270 million acres of land was made available; by 1900, 80 million acres had been taken up. The 50,000-person Oklahoma Land Rush, which opened at noon on April 22, 1889, was an example of the success of the Act. The greatest period of settlement under the Homestead Act took place between 1911 and 1915, when 42,539,903 acres were settled.

The 1814 Battle of Baltimore, which contributed so much to America's freedom to "go West," left the United States with another legacy. In 1813, a flagmaker, Mary Pickersgill, was commissioned to make two flags for Fort McHenry. After the battle the following year, American soldiers raised the garrison flag, which measured 30 feet by 42 feet, to celebrate their victory. The flag's "broad stripes and bright stars" flying "in dawn's early light" were witnessed by an attorney and amateur poet, Francis Scott Key, inspiring him to write "The Star-Spangled Banner." The song was declared the official national anthem in 1931; the flag that inspired it has been on display in the Smithsonian Institution since 1912.

Mexican-American War (1846–48). The annexation of this huge area of largely unorganized territory, together with the Gadsden Purchase in 1853 of an additional 30,000 square miles of northern Mexican territory, completed continental expansion of the United States from east to west (Alaska was acquired from Russia in 1867).

News of the Californian gold discovery traveled fast and the rush began almost immediately. President Polk confirmed the discovery in his State of the Union Address on December 5; by the end of 1848, around 5,000 prospectors were already mining in California. The following year, thousands of "49ers" arrived in San Francisco, most risking everything they had in order to get there and many dying en route or of cholera in the miners' camps. That year, $200 million of gold was mined from the hills of California, but the rush was short-lived; surface gold played out within a year or two, after which complex mining techniques were required. Further notable gold rushes took place in the Black Hills of Dakota

Mary Pickersgill made the original Star-Spangled Banner in 1813, and the flag inspired Francis Scott Key to write America's national anthem when he saw it raised over Fort McHenry after the Battle of Baltimore.

CIVIL WAR

When civil war broke out on April 12, 1861, it was the culmination of a long and progressively more bitter disagreement over the issue of slavery in the United States. The import of slaves from Africa began almost as soon as the European colonists arrived—the Spanish and Portuguese brought slaves to replace the rapidly diminishing Native American population, and in 1619 the Jamestown settlers purchased slaves from a Dutch ship, who became the first permanent African settlers in North America. They were described as "indentured servants," which in theory meant they were released after a certain period of time; in practice, however, they and their descendants were enslaved for life.

In 1641, the Massachusetts colony became the first to legalize slavery, stating in its Body of Liberties, "There shall never be any bond slavery, villeinage, or captivity amongst us . . . ," but immediately justifying slavery by continuing, ". . . unless it be lawful captives taken in just wars, and such strangers as willingly sell themselves or are sold to us." In 1670, an amendment declared "the enslavement of a slave woman's offspring to be a legal slave." Other colonies followed Massachusetts' lead, although Rhode Island declared in 1651 that an enslaved person must be freed after ten years of service.

The first antislavery protests came from the Quakers, whose English founder, George Fox, visited North America in 1671; slavery was prohibited in the Quaker settlement of West New Jersey in 1676 and in 1688 Quakers in Germantown petitioned against the practice. Quaker publications on the subject included Anthony Benezet's *Observations on the Inslaving, Importing and Purchasing of Negroes* (1759), in which he noted that "without purchasers,

The son of French Huguenots, Anthony Benezet emigrated to Pennsylvania in 1731 and founded the Commonwealth's first antislavery society. His *Observations on the Inslaving, Importing and Purchasing of Negroes* became an influential tract after it was published by Christopher Sauer, the most important German printer in colonial Pennsylvania.

there would be no trade; and consequently every purchaser . . . becomes partaker of the guilt of it." Benezet also founded the first free day school for African Americans (1770) and the world's first antislavery society "for the Relief of Free Negroes Unlawfully Held in Bondage" (1775), reorganized in 1787 as the Pennsylvania Abolition Society (PAS). Some of the Founding Fathers also became involved in the abolitionist movement—membership of the Society for Promoting the Manumission of Slaves, founded in New York in 1785, included Alexander Hamilton and John Jay, and Benjamin Franklin served briefly as president of the PAS, of which Benjamin Rush was also a member and later president.

In the South, an antislavery petition was presented in 1739 in Georgia by Scottish settlers, expressing the view that "it is shocking to human Nature, that any Race of Mankind and their Posterity should be sentanc'd to perpetual Slavery." The petition went unnoticed, however; in 1750, Georgia became the last British colony to legalize slavery.

Abolitionism in the North began in 1777, when Vermont abolished slavery in its constitution, followed by New Hampshire and Massachusetts in 1783. In 1780, Pennsylvania passed a "gradual emancipation" law; Rhode Island and Connecticut adopted similar laws in 1784, New York in 1799, and New Jersey in 1804. The Southern states, however, relied heavily on slave labor, and Eli Whitney's invention of the cotton gin in 1791, while hugely beneficial for the growing economy, promoted the rapid expansion of slavery.

Thomas Clarkson's influential *Essay on the Slavery and Commerce of the Human Species, Particularly the African* was published in London in 1786 and quickly

Painter Charles T. Webber depicts abolitionists assisting escaped slaves from the South on their journey to safe havens in the North or Canada in *The Underground Railroad* (c. 1893).

reached the U.S. The following year, the Northwest Ordinance banned the expansion of slavery north of the Ohio River, and the Constitution set 1808 as the earliest date for the federal government to ban the slave trade. In February 1790, Franklin signed a petition on behalf of the PAS, urging Congress "to countenance the Restoration of liberty to those unhappy Men, who alone, in this land of Freedom, are degraded into perpetual Bondage. . . ." The petition implied that Congress could abolish slavery before the appointed date of 1808 under the Constitution's general welfare clause. In the debate that ensued, the petition was strongly opposed by the representatives of South Carolina and especially Georgia, whose Congressman James Jackson argued vociferously for slavery in the South. The debate was tabled soon after Franklin's death in April 1790, without reaching a conclusion.

In 1793, the first Fugitive Slave Act was passed, providing for the seizure and return between states of escaped slaves, and for judgment to be passed without trial by jury. In response, some of the Northern states enacted personal-liberty laws providing for trial by jury for fugitives who appealed their sentence. The Act also gave rise to the Underground Railroad, which assisted escaped slaves from the South to reach safe havens in the North or Canada. Its activities were carried out in secret ("underground"), and the stopping points were called "stations," the helpers "conductors," and the escapees "freight" (hence "railroad").

In 1794, a number of antislavery societies united to form the American Convention for Promoting the Abolition of Slavery. The African Americans also initiated their own movement—in 1797, for example, free blacks in Philadelphia petitioned Congress to protest North Carolina laws re-enslaving blacks freed during the Revolution, and in 1800 Absalom Jones and others petitioned against the slave trade and the Fugitive Slave Act.

On January 1, 1808, the African slave trade was abolished under the Act Prohibiting Importation of Slaves (1807). By this time, most Northern states had abolished slavery; however, the practice was still prevalent in the South, and the Act did not prohibit the slave trade within the Southern states. As westward expansion progressed following the 1803 Louisiana Purchase, tensions between North and South began to escalate over the "slave" or "free" status of newly created states. Matters almost reached crisis point in 1820, when the new slave state of Missouri sought admission to the Union, triggering fears of a Senate imbalance in favor of the pro-slavery states. The solution was the Missouri Compromise, which created Maine as a free state. It also provided that all new states below the 36°30' parallel (the southern border of Missouri) would permit slavery, while those above would prohibit it. Thomas Jefferson later wrote that he considered the Missouri question "the knell of the Union."

In 1829, the black abolitionist David Walker published his *Appeal in Four Articles . . . to the Coloured Citizens of the World*, a warning to white Americans of an impending slave revolt if slavery were not abolished. The Southern states promptly passed legislation prohibiting circulation

Painter James Walker's *Gettysburg, The First Day* (1863) was one of the first depictions of the action between McPherson's Ridge and Seminary Ridge from 2:30–3:00 PM on July 1, 1863.

of abolitionist literature. In 1831, the antislavery newspaper *The Liberator* was founded by William Lloyd Garrison, who also became leader of the American Antislavery Society, formed in 1833. In 1845, publication of Frederick Douglass's *Narrative of the Life of Frederick Douglass, an American Slave* launched him as a leader of the abolition movement.

In 1854, the Kansas–Nebraska Act repealed the 1820 Missouri Compromise prohibiting slavery north of 36°30', leading to "Bleeding Kansas," a violent conflict between free-soil forces from the North and pro-slavery advocates from the South for control of the new territory of Kansas under the doctrine of popular sovereignty. This empowered the occupants of federal lands to decide whether their territories would enter the Union as free or slave states. Kansas was eventually admitted as a free state in 1861.

In 1856, the Republican Party, newly formed from groups opposing the extension of slavery, held its first convention in Philadelphia. The name was coined by newspaper magnate Horace Greeley, who observed that "some simple name like 'Republican' would . . . fitly designate those who had united to restore the Union to its true

mission of champion and promulgator of Liberty. . . ." The following year, the Supreme Court's Dred Scott decision ruled that African Americans, whether free or slave, had no citizenship rights.

On November 6, 1860, Abraham Lincoln was elected the first Republican president. In response, the Southern states seceded from the Union and, in February 1861, formed the Confederate States of America, with Jefferson Davis as president. Their aim was to preserve slavery, states' rights, and political liberty for white Americans. The Lincoln administration and most of the Northern states refused to acknowledge the secession and the first battle of the Civil War began when Confederate warships bombarded Union soldiers at Fort Sumter, South Carolina.

As a Republican, Lincoln was committed to excluding slavery from the territories in anticipation of "ultimate

Top: A photograph of Dred Scott, around the time of his court case in 1857.

Above: On March 4, 1865, President Abraham Lincoln gave his second inaugural address, on the east portico of the U.S. Capitol.

The White House copy of George Peter Alexander Healy's lost painting *The Peacemakers* (1868), which depicts Sherman, Grant, Lincoln, and Porter aboard the steamer River Queen on March 27–28, 1865.

extinction." However, the Constitution obliged him to protect slavery where it was wanted. His motivation for the war was thus primarily concerned with keeping the Union together, but the issue of slavery was very much the underlying factor. On September 22, 1862, he issued a preliminary Emancipation Proclamation, declaring that from January 1, 1863, all slaves in the rebellious Southern states would be "then, thenceforward, and forever free." At that point, African American volunteers entered the war; the Army was also supplemented through conscription.

The bloodiest battle of the war, and in North American history, was Gettysburg, which began on July 1, 1863, when Confederate soldiers led by Robert E. Lee met General Meade's Union Army. The three-day battle ended in Confederate defeat; 51,000 soldiers had been killed, wounded, captured, or were missing. On November 19,

1863, Lincoln delivered the Gettysburg Address at the dedication of the National Cemetery on the site of the battle.

The final battle, at Palmito Ranch, Texas, took place on May 12, 1865. The Confederate force won the battle, but elsewhere, the Confederates had already signed surrender documents, and Jefferson Davis had been captured on May 10 at Irwinville, Georgia. The South was in ruins; six of the states were readmitted to the Union by August 1868 and the remaining states in 1870.

The Thirteenth Amendment to the Constitution, which formally abolished the institution of slavery, was adopted on December 6, 1865. It was not the end of the African Americans' problems, however; supremacist organizations such as the Ku Klux Klan were formed, and slavery was very soon replaced by segregation and other systematic forms of discrimination.

The Progressive Era

etween the end of the post-Civil War Reconstruction Era in 1877 and the turn of the century, more than ten million immigrants entered the United States, followed by almost fifteen million more between 1901 and 1920. This huge influx, together with the shift to urban occupations as technological innovations lured the existing workforce into the industrial centers, resulted in overcrowding and poor living and working conditions.

When Roosevelt took office in 1901, the country had just emerged from the second of two major economic depressions—the Panics of 1873 (1873–79) and 1893 (1893–97)—and was moving into a phase of rapid growth. Corruption was rife in industry and politics, and a disgruntled workforce was expressing its dissatisfaction through strikes. For some, the late 1800s were a "Gilded Age" synonymous with the acquisition of extraordinary wealth. A handful of "captains of industry" from that era stand out as the men who shaped modern America. Cornelius Vanderbilt was an industrialist in railroads and shipping; by his death in 1877, he had acquired the largest fortune in the U.S. to date. John D. Rockefeller made his money in oil, Andrew Carnegie in steel, and J. P. Morgan in finance. However, while the big companies that created the multimillionaires flourished, their business practices were often ruthless and to the detriment of smaller companies, which either struggled to survive or were absorbed or forced out of business.

Roosevelt therefore undertook to redress the balance. One of his first measures was to prosecute a recently formed railroad trust, the Northern Securities Company, under the Sherman Antitrust Act (1890). The Act had been passed to prohibit monopolistic business practices, specifically Rockefeller's control of the oil industry. Rockefeller founded the Standard Oil Company in 1870, and within ten years not only dominated oil refining in the U.S., but had also acquired other businesses associated with its production and distribution. In 1882 he organized his empire into the Standard Oil Trust, America's first multinational corporation.

THE JUNGLE

UPTON SINCLAIR

The heart of the Great Union Stock Yards, Chicago's meatpacking district (c. 1909).

The success of Standard Oil's business model inspired the formation of trusts in other major industries, such as railroads, coal, steel, sugar, and meat-packing. While the practice was extremely popular with the trustees and shareholders, it was decidedly less so with those whose businesses were adversely affected. It also caught the attention of the media, who kept an increasingly appalled public fully informed and launched a "muckraking" attack on monopolistic practice and the associated corruption. The muckrakers' relentless exposure of malpractice did much toward prompting the reforms of the Progressive Era; for example, Lincoln Steffens' book *The Shame of the Cities* exposed corruption of politicians by businessmen seeking special privileges, while Upton Sinclair's novel *The Jungle* (1906), based on Chicago's meat-packing industry, led to the passage of the Meat Inspection and Pure Food and Drug Acts (1906).

Despite the anger directed at the trusts, the Sherman Antitrust Act was rarely used before Roosevelt's presidency. It was in any case largely ineffective—when the Standard Oil Trust was dissolved under the Act in 1892, the trustees simply reorganized in 1899 as the Standard Oil Company of New Jersey (where the laws permitted a parent company to own the stock of other companies). In 1904, the journalist Ida

An initially peaceful labor protest in Chicago turns into a full-scale riot when protesters throw a bomb and police indiscriminately fire into the mostly unarmed crowd, during the Haymarket Riot on May 4, 1886.

Tarbell published a book called *The History of the Standard Oil Company,* essentially an exposé of the company, which was eventually ordered to dissolve in 1911.

While the big industries were expanding, the Labor Movement was also underway to protect the interests of the workforce. In 1869, the Knights of Labor (KOL) was founded, America's first major national labor organization. Membership of KOL increased after the Great Railroad Strike of 1877, the first general strike in U.S. history, which was triggered by wage cuts resulting from the 1873 Panic and ended with intervention by federal troops. However, in 1886 KOL was held responsible for the Haymarket Riot in Chicago, which began as peaceful local participation in a national campaign to secure an eight-hour workday, but ended in violent confrontation when a bomb was lobbed at police. The event became a symbol of the international struggle for workers' rights. Membership of KOL declined and in December 1886, Samuel Gompers established the American Federation of Labor which, unlike KOL, represented autonomous craft unions rather than a single national union, and focused on gaining economic benefits through collective bargaining. Further industrial action included a protest march on Washington in 1894 by unemployed Ohio workers, known as Coxey's Army after their leader, Jacob Coxey, and a five-month strike by anthracite coal miners in 1902. This threatened the closure of schools and hospitals, prompting Roosevelt to mediate and achieve a "Square Deal" between capital and labor. He used the term as his slogan in the 1904 election.

Meanwhile, in 1892, a coalition of agrarian reformers organized the People's (or Populist) Party to represent the interests of farmers and laborers. The Omaha Platform, which set out their mission, advocated public ownership of railroads, a graduated federal income tax, and unlimited coinage of silver. Although the party was short-lived, some of its aims were later adopted by Roosevelt's Progressive Party. However, the railroads became the first industry to be subject to federal regulation, under the Interstate Commerce Commission created by the Interstate Commerce Act (1887). The Hepburn Act (1906) extended the Commission's powers to include regulation of interstate railroad rates.

Roosevelt's progressive policy also extended to conservation. He established five national parks—Crater Lake in 1902, Wind Cave in 1903, Sullys Hill in 1904, and Mesa Verde (now also a World Heritage Site) and Platt (now part of Chickasaw National Recreation Area) in 1906—and created the Forest Service in 1905 to manage forest reserves created under the Forest Management Act (1897), and set aside 194 million acres of public land as national forests to be protected from commercial exploitation.

President Theodore Roosevelt delivers a speech in Evanston, Illinois, in 1903.

In 1912, having split with the Republicans, Roosevelt formed the Progressive Party; however, both Taft and Roosevelt were defeated in the 1912 election by the Democrat Woodrow Wilson. Wilson's vision of progressivism was to break down the "Triple Wall of Privilege"—tariffs, banks, and trusts—and achieve a "New Freedom" in favor of small farmers and businesses. He first passed the United States Revenue Act (1913), or Underwood Tariff, which significantly reduced duties on foreign goods. The Federal Reserve Act (1913) created a decentralized national banking system, with the Federal Reserve System as the central authority. The Clayton Antitrust Act (1914) reinforced the Sherman Act and allowed the punishment of monopolistic corporations, while the Federal Trade Commission was created in 1914 to prevent unfair or deceptive trade practices and enforce antitrust and consumer protection legislation. The Clayton Act also legalized labor unions and their right to strike peacefully. Further measures to protect the workforce included the

La Follette Seaman's Act (1915), the Federal Farm Loan and Warehouse Acts (1916), the Workingmen's Compensation Act (1916), and the Adamson Act (1916), which established an eight-hour workday for employees on interstate railroads.

When World War I broke out in Europe in 1914, the United States remained neutral at first, although the nation

Above, inset: Published by the Recruiting Committee of the Mayor's Committee on National Defense, this poster encourages citizens to respond to the call to duty.

Above: Soldiers about to sail to France aboard the USS *Hancock* (c. 1917).

VOTES FOR WOMEN PROCESSION
...AYETTE SQUARE TO CAPITOL
...ATURDAY MAY 9
STARTS 3 P.M.
PRECEDED BY
...EETING BELASCO TH...
$1 75¢ 50¢ 25¢ | 12,30 O'CLOCK P.M. | REGISTER
...D F ST.

Suffragists use banners at the White House to promote the right for women to vote.

was shocked when German submarines sank the British Cunard liner *Lusitania*, whose passenger list included 128 Americans, in May 1915. However, in January 1917, British cryptographers deciphered a telegram from the German Foreign Minister Arthur Zimmerman to the German Minister to Mexico, authorizing the proposal of an alliance with Mexico in return for financial support that would enable Mexico to reconquer territory lost to the U.S. in the Mexican–American War (1846–48). The British notified Wilson of the telegram on February 24 and Congress declared war on Germany on April 6. Under the Selective Service Act (1917), nearly three million men were conscripted into the Army over the remainder of the war. After the war, the U.S. wished to maintain an isolationist foreign policy and thus did not join the new League of Nations.

A final achievement of the Progressive Era was the ratification of the Nineteenth Amendment, granting women's suffrage. The first Women's Rights convention was held in 1848, setting the agenda for the movement. Women then played a significant role in the Civil War—some assumed responsibility for running their households, while others nursed the wounded, and a small number even fought, disguised as men. Spurred by the passage in 1869 of the Fifteenth Amendment, which granted African American men the right to vote, the National Woman Suffrage and American Woman Suffrage associations were formed that year, focused on gaining voting rights through a Constitutional amendment and individual state constitutions, respectively. The two groups merged in 1890 to form the National American Woman Suffrage Association (NAWSA) and launched state-by-state campaigns; between 1893 and 1918, sixteen states adopted amendments. In 1913, the Congressional Union, later the National Women's Party, was formed; to raise their profile, members engaged in acts of civil disobedience, including picketing the White House. The Nineteenth Amendment was passed in 1919 and ratified on August 18, 1920; and the Roaring Twenties would become an era of liberation for women.

THE ROARING TWENTIES

America entered the 1920s in an unsettled frame of mind. At the end of the previous decade, the U.S. had engaged in a war it had expected to avoid, in which nearly 117,000 American soldiers died in battle or through disease or accidents, and over 200,000 were wounded. By the end of the war, millions of Americans, including women, were employed in war-related industries—jobs that ended with the Armistice, resulting in unemployment, recession, and strikes. After the war, an estimated 675,000 U.S. citizens died in the influenza pandemic of 1918–19; and the Russian Revolution in 1917 provoked a fear of communism in the U.S., leading to a brief but extreme "Red Scare" in 1919 that left Americans with a distrust of all foreigners. As presidential candidate Warren G. Harding summed up the mood in May 1920: "America's present need is not heroics, but healing; not nostrums, but normalcy; . . . not submergence in internationality, but sustainment in triumphant nationality."

During his term in office, which was cut short by his death in 1923, Harding dedicated himself to the growth of business. Although both Harding and his successor, Calvin Coolidge, adopted a policy of "laissez-faire" (allowing the economy the freedom to develop itself), the process was assisted with spectacular success in the mid to late 1920s by the Secretary of the Treasury, Andrew W. Mellon. The Secretary had cofounded the Aluminum Company of America (Alcoa) in 1886 and the Gulf Oil Corporation in 1901, and was one of the world's richest men. As Secretary of the Treasury, Mellon cut federal spending to help reduce the national debt, but more importantly he initiated tax cuts, which promoted rapid economic growth by encouraging wealthy taxpayers to reinvest in business.

Between 1913, when the Sixteenth Amendment established the graduated federal income tax, and the end of the war, the top rate of tax increased from 7 percent to 73 percent. Under the Revenue Acts of 1921, 1924, and 1926,

John Held's illustration, "Teaching Old Dogs New Tricks," for the February 1926 cover of *Life* magazine shows that flappers and the Charleston were at the height of style.

the top rates were cut back in phases to 25 percent. Industrial output doubled, and because the tax cuts resulted in a higher level of disposable income, sales of consumer goods, especially cars and electrical items, increased greatly. American consumerism was also facilitated by the introduction of cheap and efficient mass production, shopping catalogs, and installment plans; and while the U.S. was able to dominate the European market, which was still in a state of postwar recovery, the purchase of foreign imports by the American public was discouraged through the Fordney-McCumber Tariff Act (1922), which significantly increased import duties. As the *Wall Street Journal* observed, "No government ever before . . . has succeeded in uniting so thoroughly with the business world."

For many people, then, the Twenties were indeed Roaring and America's young society, in particular, embraced the new era. They eagerly adopted the creative output of the Harlem Renaissance—literary, theatrical, and visual arts as well as jazz—that characterized the 1920s and beyond. Fashions moved into the modern age—young men abandoned the frock coat, stiff collar, and top hat in favor of lounge suits for business, while casual clothing mirrored that worn by sport stars, such as golfing knickerbockers or white flannel tennis trousers. Women, too, many of whom had gained an unprecedented level of social and economic independence through employment during the war, made full use of the emancipation granted under the Nineteenth Amendment. Before the war, the "Gibson Girl"—a young lady with an hourglass figure, upswept hair, a long skirt, and high collar, created in the imagination of illustrator Charles Dana Gibson—had represented the feminine ideal. In contrast, the quintessential 1920s "flapper" had a boyish, uncorseted figure, bobbed her hair, wore short dresses with daring necklines, and danced the Charleston with a slender cigarette holder in her hand. Chaperones

Joe "King" Oliver and his Creole Jazz Band revolutionized jazz music and were immensely popular in the early 1920s.

The exuberance of the Roaring Twenties was muted by the fact that it was also the Prohibition Era. The Eighteenth Amendment, passed in December 1917 and ratified in January 1919, prohibited the "manufacture, sale, or transportation of intoxicating liquors within, the importation thereof into, or the exportation thereof from the United States." The American Temperance Movement began as early as 1808 in Saratoga, N.Y., its proponents firmly believing that consumption of alcohol was the cause of many of society's ills, especially crime, poverty, and immorality. The initial view that moderation was acceptable quickly gave way to a conviction that teetotalism was the goal. The movement grew rapidly, supported by the various churches. The virtues and benefits of temperance were promoted in hymns, poetry, and art, and in humorous popular songs,

became a thing of the past, and in 1923, Alice Reighly organized the Anti-Flirt Club in Washington, D.C., which issued a set of guidelines to protect flappers from inappropriate advances by men. The first rule was: "Don't flirt; those who flirt in haste often repent in leisure."

The 1920s were, however, a period of sexual liberation for women. In 1914, the campaigner Margaret Sanger, who is credited with coining the term "birth control," published *The Woman Rebel*, a magazine about contraception, and in 1916 she opened America's first birth-control clinic, in Brooklyn. Her arrest and subsequent imprisonment under the Comstock Act (1873), which banned the distribution of birth control information and devices through the mail, generated public support for her campaign. She founded the American Birth Control League in 1921 and the National Committee for Federal Legislation on Birth Control in 1928. Meanwhile, Julia Lathrop, the first director of the Children's Bureau formed in 1912, had campaigned for federal funding for maternity and infant care programs, which became available under the Sheppard-Towner Act (1921).

The Gay Rights movement also began tentatively in the 1920s with the foundation in 1924 of the first recognized gay rights association, the Society for Human Rights, by a German immigrant, Henry Gerber. The society produced *Friendship and Freedom*, the first American newsletter for homosexuals, but disbanded under political pressure soon afterward.

Margaret Sanger, a women's sexual liberation activist, opened America's first birth-control clinic in Brooklyn.

Authorities empty barrels of beer into the sewer during Prohibition.

usually written by women, for women—the chorus of one song urged girls to "wait for a Temperance man./A teetotaler if you can./For your life will be bright/And your purse never light/If you wait for a Temperance man."

The first state prohibition legislation was passed in Maine in 1846 and by 1855 a further thirteen states had enacted similar legislation. In 1869 the National Prohibition Party was founded, the oldest minor U.S. political party still in existence; it polled 2.2 percent of the vote in the presidential elections of 1888 and 1892. In 1893, the Anti-Saloon League was founded in Ohio; it soon became the leading organization lobbying for prohibition and led to a series of state prohibitions between 1906 and 1913. The movement was supported by the Woman's Christian Temperance Union (WCTU), founded in 1874, which soon became the largest women's organization in U.S. history, with around 250,000 members. In 1917, the National Prohibition Act

(Volstead Act) was passed to provide enforcement for the Eighteenth Amendment; its provisions included a war-time prohibition to save grain.

When prohibition finally came into effect, it failed to produce the desired results. Although it was enforced, this tended only to be in rural areas and small towns, where the cause had always been supported. In the big cities, where enforcement was needed, it was far weaker. A bigger problem, however, was the practice of bootlegging—the illegal production, distribution, and sale of liquor—which quickly became a major criminal activity. A popular venue for the purchase of illicit liquor was a "speakeasy," such as New York's 21 Club, Cotton Club, and Stork Club. Cunning methods were devised to foil police raids—customers left hastily by an alternate exit and the 21 Club, for example, had a secret passageway leading to a cellar beneath an adjacent building, where the illicit liquor was stored on shelves that could be remotely tipped by the barman in the event of a raid, so that the bottles slid off into the sewer system and smashed.

Bootlegging led to the creation of organized gangs, or "mobs," which merged to form monopolies such as the Mafia and extended their operations to include narcotics trafficking and gambling, prostitution, and labor racketeering, as well as loan-sharking and extortion. The most notorious mobster was Al Capone, who operated in Chicago and ruthlessly gunned down rival gangs in cold blood; he was believed to be responsible for the St. Valentine's Day Massacre (1929), when gangsters disguised as policemen lined up seven members of an opposing gang against a garage wall and shot them. In the meantime, Capone had amassed a fortune estimated at around $100,000,000; he was tried for income-tax evasion in 1931 and imprisoned, his reign of terror at an end. Congress recognized that prohibition had failed and the Twenty-First Amendment, ratified on December 5, 1933, repealed the Eighteenth Amendment. To date, the Eighteenth is the only amendment to have been repealed.

Another murky aspect of the 1920s was the revival of the Ku Klux Klan. The organization was founded in 1866, in the wake of the Civil War, by Confederate veterans in the South, but disbanded in the 1870s. However, in 1915 a silent movie called *The Birth of a Nation* was released, based on Thomas Dixon's novel *The Clansman* and directed by D. W. Griffith. The film glorified the activities of the Ku Klux Klan, and while attempts to ban the film were made by the National Association for the Advancement of Colored People (NAACP), the African American civil rights organization founded in 1909, the Ku Klux Klan used it to launch a huge recruiting campaign in June 1920, which attracted millions of new members. The Klan extended its supremacist activities to target Catholics and Jews, both of whom now had large populations in the U.S., as well as foreigners in general, elite society, and, of course, African Americans—anyone, in fact, who did not match their perception of "clean living." The Klan also initiated a "decade" strategy, which required each member to recruit ten people to vote for Klan candidates in local and state elections. Although the organization continued

to exist well beyond the 1920s, its activities had peaked.

F. Scott Fitzgerald's novel *The Great Gatsby* epitomizes the wild excesses of the Roaring Twenties. When the book was published in 1925, America had no notion that the decade would end with the Wall Street Crash, the worst stock market crash in history, less than two months after the market reached an all-time high.

Below left: A roll of ticker tape from the stock market crash in October 1929.

Below: After the stock market crashed, 400 extra police officers were dispatched to protect the Financial District as crowds of worried and angry pedestrians flooded Wall Street.

THE GREAT DEPRESSION

This is an example of a Civilian Conservation Corps patch.

By the end of the 1920s, the economic boom was coming to an end. Supply of consumer goods had reached the point of exceeding demand; the profligacy of a throw-away society had yet to emerge, and in any case a number of factors resulted in a decrease in available disposable income—for example, developments in technology led to unemployment as machinery replaced the workforce in certain industries, while a fall in real estate values after 1926 left many experiencing negative equity and foreclosure. Companies that provided installment-plan facilities faced financial difficulties as customers were unable to honor their debts. Finally, attempts to offload surplus industrial and agricultural output into Europe failed as European countries had imposed a tax on American goods in retaliation for duties on foreign imports imposed by the Fordney–McCumber Tariff Act (1922).

Despite this, the stock market was in an extremely robust state at the end of the 1920s. Stock prices rose sharply in 1927, and 1928 saw an unprecedented boom as the benefits of short-term investment were recognized. Even speculators without the capital to pay the full price were able to buy on margin through brokers such as small banks. Confidence in the stability of the stock market was so great that by the height of the boom over 20 million people had invested. A minor crash in March 1929 and subsequent warnings of the economic downturn were ignored, and on September 3 the Dow Jones Industrial Average closed at 381.17, an all-time high. However, investment faltered over the next two months, and on October 24 plummeting prices caused a flurry of panic selling of nearly 13 million shares. Reinvestment by a group of bankers restored confidence, but only momentarily; on October 29—Black Tuesday—over 16 million more shares were sold. Speculators lost all their financial assets: banks and companies closed, and the devastation left by the Wall Street Crash, together with the already weakened economy, resulted in the Great Depression of the 1930s.

The effects of the crash reached far beyond the shores of the U.S. On June 17, 1930, Congress increased the import tariff under the United States (Smoot–Hawley) Tariff Act; however, far from benefitting American businesses and farmers, the Act served only to reinforce the hostility engendered by the Fordney–McCumber Act, provoke further retaliatory legislation, and promote American isolationism. It also triggered a trend of isolationist policy elsewhere, weakening the global economy. International cooperation in trade was not resumed until the introduction of the reciprocal trade program under the Reciprocal Trade Agreement Act (1934).

When it came to the next election, therefore, the cry of the American voters was "In Hoover we trusted, now we are busted!" The 1932 election was the third "critical" election in U.S. history—the first was the 1860 election of Lincoln that prompted the secession of the Southern states, and the second the 1896 election of McKinley, when many voters switched allegiance to the Republican Party, fearing that the Democrats' proposed monetary policy based on silver instead of gold would lead to high inflation. In

Franklin Delano Roosevelt and Herbert Hoover ride in a convertible on their way to Roosevelt's inauguration at the U.S. Capitol on March 4, 1933.

1932, with blame for the Depression laid firmly at the feet of the Republicans, voting swung back in favor of the Democrats, and Franklin D. Roosevelt (FDR), a distant cousin of Theodore, won the election by a landslide.

When FDR took office on March 4, 1933, he inherited the leadership of a nation in which an average of nearly 25 percent was unemployed; the percentage was higher in the industrial cities, where many were homeless and were being fed in soup kitchens. Some camped in hastily constructed shacktowns, collectively known as "Hooverville." In rural areas, where poverty rather than wealth had been prevalent throughout the 1920s owing to overproduction, many farmers were either indebted to their banks or forced to sell while their crops rotted in grain bins. Teenage boys, and even some girls, became hoboes to relieve the burden on their parents, begging for food and "riding the rails," an illegal, dangerous, and often fatal mode of free transport. Hitchhiking was a legal and, to some extent, safer alternative. Between 1933 and 1935, Transient Bureaus were established to provide emergency relief for hoboes in the main cities and along the main travel routes.

In his inauguration speech, FDR assured America that "This great nation will survive, as it has survived. It will recover and become rich again. . . . I believe that the only thing we have to fear is fear itself." His cabinet was sworn in without ceremony and his immediate task was to address the banking crisis and restore confidence with the first of a series of New Deal measures. On March 5, FDR halted trading in gold and declared a four-day national "bank holiday," effectively closing the banks while Congress passed an Emergency Banking Bill that would authorize government to reorganize and reopen solvent banks. On March 12, FDR broadcast a "fireside chat" on radio—the first of many— to reassure the nation that the banking crisis was over and that their deposits were safe; and when the first banks reopened the following day, deposits exceeded withdrawals. On April 5, in order to increase federal gold reserves and inflate money supply, FDR ordered all gold, bullion, and certificates to be turned in and exchanged for other currency; on June 5, the U.S. suspended the gold standard.

Between March 9 and June 16, 1933, known as the "Hundred Days" session, FDR enacted fifteen major laws,

A fifteen year old and a sixteen year old ride the freights along with an older hobo in San Joaquin Valley, California, in 1940.

delivered fifteen messages and ten speeches to Congress, which he kept in special session, and held regular press conferences and cabinet meetings. He was assisted by a group of academic and other advisors, who were dubbed the Brain Trust. Further measures to support consumer confidence in the revitalized banking system included the Banking (Glass–Steagall) Act, passed on June 16. The Act established the Federal Deposit Insurance Corporation (FDIC), which separated commercial from investment banking, assumed responsibility for insuring small deposits in eligible banks against loss in the event of a further failure, and regulated banking practices. The Securities Exchange Act (1934) created the Securities and Exchange Commission to prevent misleading sales practices and stock manipulations, thereby restoring investor confidence in the stock market.

With the banking crisis stabilized, FDR began to implement measures to address the economic and social effects of the Depression. The National Industrial Recovery Act (1933) created the National Recovery Administration to promote the establishment and enforcement of codes governing prices and wages, while labor was offered protection from unfair practices and granted the right to collective bargaining. This was reinforced under the Second New Deal by the National Labor Relations (Wagner) Act (1935), which established the federal government as regulator and arbiter of labor relations and created the National Labor Relations Board to protect workers' rights to organize unions, and to encourage collective bargaining. In 1938, the Fair Labor Standards (Wages and Hours) Act, applied to all industries engaged in interstate commerce, established a minimum wage and compensation for overtime.

On March 31, 1933, Congress established the Civilian Conservation Corps (CCC) which, over its nine-year existence, provided employment for more than three million young men in natural resource conservation. Roosevelt's "Tree Army" planted an estimated three billion trees, maintained access roads, re-seeded grazing lands, and constructed wildlife refuges, fish-rearing facilities, water storage basins, bridges, and camping facilities. The CCC also implemented soil-erosion controls; this was particularly important in the Great Plains "Dust Bowl," the result of poor agricultural practices in the 1920s, when small-scale wheat farmers ploughed in the native grasses, destroying the protective cover that retained moisture in the soil. When drought hit the region in the 1930s, dry winds blew the exposed topsoil into billowing black clouds. A Dust Bowl storm is one of the enduring images of the Great Depression; the devastation is described in John Steinbeck's *The Grapes of Wrath*, published in 1939.

Dorothea Lange, preeminent documentary photographer of the Depression, shows a poor mother and children in Elm Grove, Oklahoma, in 1936.

On May 12, 1933, the Federal Emergency Relief Act established the Federal Emergency Relief Administration, authorized to distribute federal aid to the states. By the end of 1935, the agency had distributed over $3 billion and employed more than twenty million people on projects set up by, for example, the Civil Works Administration (CWA), which created construction jobs for unskilled laborers, ranging from laying

Taken from a watchtower, this photograph shows a dust storm in Rolla, Kansas, in 1935.

sewer pipes to shoveling snow in public parks. In 1935, the Emergency Relief Appropriation Act created the Works Progress Administration (WPA), which provided employment on civic construction projects. WPA sponsorship also extended to creative projects, employing artists, writers, actors, and musicians in cultural programs for community benefit, while the National Youth Administration created part-time jobs for students. The Social Security Administration, established under the Social Security Act (1935), created a permanent national old-age pension system, unemployment compensation, and federal financial support for dependents and people with disabilities.

On June 13, 1933, the Home Owners Loan Corporation (HOLC) was established, tasked with refinancing mortgages on non-farm residential properties either in default or at risk of foreclosure. The following year, the National Housing Act (1934) created the Federal Housing Administration (FHA), which insured banks, mortgage companies, and other lenders to encourage the construction of new homes. The Housing (Wagner–Steagall) Act (1937) created the United States

During the Depression, unemployed men line up outside a soup kitchen opened in Chicago by Al Capone.

Housing Authority (USHA), responsible for the construction of publicly subsidized housing. By the end of 1940, over 500 projects were in progress or had been completed.

A separate federal policy was established to assist the farming community, which by the 1930s was in a grave state. The Agricultural Adjustment Act (1933) aimed to raise prices for basic farming outputs—corn, wheat, cotton, rice, peanuts, tobacco, and milk—by balancing supply and demand. In order to achieve this, farmers were compensated for limiting production. Measures were also implemented to improve rural living standards and discourage migration into urban centers.

From January 1935, several key pieces of New Deal legislation were declared unconstitutional by conservative members of the Supreme Court on the grounds that they delegated too much authority to the federal government. In 1937, in an attempt to overcome this, FDR proposed a Judiciary Reorganization Bill, ostensibly to increase the efficiency of the judiciary. The scheme, which would enable FDR to introduce new, liberal blood to the Court by appointing one new justice for every sitting justice over the age of seventy, was highly controversial and became known as his "court-packing plan." Although the bill was not passed, FDR lost support and ironically, after all his efforts, it was ultimately the outbreak of World War II in 1939 that put the United States on the road to economic recovery.

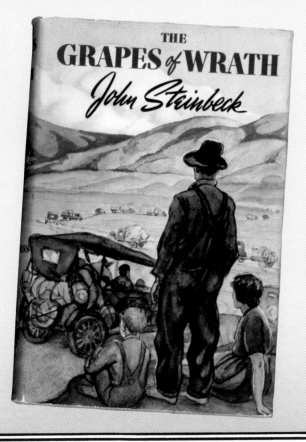

WORLD WAR II AND THE COLD WAR

While America was in the grip of the Great Depression, Europe was heading inexorably toward a second world war. On January 30, 1933, Adolf Hitler, *führer* (leader) of Germany's National Socialist Workers' (Nazi) Party, was appointed as the country's chancellor. He immediately established the Gestapo, a secret political police force, and set up concentration camps to retain opponents to his goal of transforming Germany into a unified one-party state. In 1935, the Nazi Party approved Hitler's Nuremberg Laws—the Reich Citizenship Law, depriving Jews of German citizenship, and the Blood Protection Law, prohibiting marriage or sexual relations between Jews and citizens of German or "kindred" blood. The following summer, despite calls to boycott the event, the Olympics were held in Berlin. The African American athlete Jesse Owens won four gold medals, one of which was auctioned in December 2013 for $1.46 million.

By 1938, a quarter of Germany's Jewish population had fled the country, but when Germany annexed Austria in March 1938, more Jews came under Nazi rule. The night of November 9, 1938, saw a series of Nazi attacks on Jews and their properties, including synagogues and businesses, in retaliation for the assassination in Paris of a German diplomat by a Polish-Jewish student. The pogroms, known as *Kristallnacht* or the "Night of Broken Glass," signalled the end of Jewish survival in Germany. However, the refugees had nowhere to go; the U.S., for example, had immigration quotas in place, and a Limited Refugee Bill, proposed in February 1939 to admit 20,000 German refugees under the age of fourteen to the U.S., was defeated. In June 1939, 900 refugees aboard the SS *St. Louis* were refused entry to Cuba or the U.S. and returned to Europe to face the Holocaust.

Meanwhile, Hitler and the Italian fascist dictator, Benito Mussolini, had formed an alliance. In October 1936, they signed a treaty of friendship, the Rome–Berlin Axis; this became a full military and political alliance under the Pact

Following a church service, British Prime Minister Winston Churchill and U.S. President Franklin D. Roosevelt talk aboard the British battleship *Prince of Wales* off the coast of Newfoundland during the Atlantic Conference on September 10, 1941.

of Steel, signed on May 22, 1939. Germany had also formed an alliance with Japan against the Soviet Union (USSR) under the Anti-Comintern Pact (1936). On September 30, 1938, the Munich Agreement between Germany, Britain, France, and Italy permitted German annexation of Czechoslovakia's Sudetenland, which had a high German population; but when Germany also invaded the rest of Czechoslovakia, Britain and France issued formal guarantees to protect Poland, Romania, and Greece. In August 1939, Germany and the USSR signed a nonaggression pact, which allowed Germany to invade Poland on September 1 without fear of Soviet intervention. Two days later, Britain and France declared war on Germany. On September 27, Germany, Italy, and Japan signed a Tripartite Pact, agreeing mutual assistance in the event of attack by either the U.S. or the USSR, the two powers not yet involved in the conflicts in Europe and Asia (China and Japan had been at war since July 1937).

In 1935, with events indicating the likelihood of another world war, Congress passed the first of a series of three Neutrality Acts, "an expression of the desire . . . to avoid any action which might involve [the U.S.] in war." The 1935 Act prohibited the export of arms, ammunition, and implements of war to foreign nations at war and advised Americans traveling in war zones that they did so at their own risk. An extension of the Act prohibited the granting of loans to "belligerent" nations. The 1937 Neutrality Act, passed in response to the outbreak of the Spanish Civil War and the rise of fascism in Europe, forbade U.S. citizens to travel on belligerent ships, prohibited the transportation of arms on American merchant ships to belligerent nations (including nations in a state of civil war), authorized the President to bar all belligerent ships from U.S. waters, and extended the export embargo to include "articles or materials" of war. However, the Act also carried a "cash and carry" clause, allowing the sale for cash of any items that did not fall into the category of "arms" or "implements of war," as long as the items were carried on non-American ships. The clause was intended to assist Britain and France with the provision of materials in the event of any war against the Axis Powers—Germany, Italy, and Japan. The third Neutrality Act, passed in November 1939, extended this clause to include arms.

Although the U.S. theoretically remained neutral at this point, FDR now began to implement other measures to assist the British. After the heroic evacuation of the British Expeditionary Force and allied troops from Dunkirk in 1940, for example, the U.S. War and Navy departments resupplied the troops with weaponry. Following an unprecedented third election victory in 1940, FDR then proposed the Lend-Lease Act, passed by Congress in March 1941, which authorized the provision of aid to any nation whose

defense was believed vital to the security of the U.S. in exchange for repayment "in kind," so that Britain was no longer required to pay cash. The lend-lease system was later extended to China and the USSR. In his Annual Message to Congress on January 6, 1941, FDR explained his rationale for supporting Britain in the "Four Freedoms" speech. The Freedoms—freedom of speech and worship, and freedom from want and fear—are illustrated in Norman Rockwell's *The Four Freedoms* series of oil paintings (1943), and the speech is commemorated in the Four Freedoms Park opened on Roosevelt Island, New York City, in 2012.

On August 14, 1941, FDR and the British Prime Minister, Winston Churchill, signed the Atlantic Charter, a statement of their common aims during and after the war with regard to issues such as sovereignty, trade, and disarmament. The U.S. entered the war at the end of 1941. On December 7, a day that FDR said would "live in infamy," Japanese aircraft launched a surprise attack on the U.S. Pacific Fleet moored at Pearl Harbor on the Hawaiian island of Oahu, sinking five battleships and destroying 188 aircraft. The Japanese wished to disable the U.S. fleet so they could invade Southeast Asia unchallenged; instead, the U.S. declared war on Japan the following day, and on December 11, Japan's allies, Germany and Italy, declared war on the U.S. On January 1, 1942,

SAVE FREEDOM OF SPEECH

BUY WAR BONDS

Left: Norman Rockwell's World War II poster Freedom of Speech is the first in his Four Freedoms series inspired by President Franklin D. Roosevelt's State of the Union Address of January 6, 1941. The illustration appeared in *The Saturday Evening Post* on February 20, 1943.

Below: USS *Shaw* (DD-373) blows up during the Imperial Japanese Navy's surprise raid on the U.S. naval base Pearl Harbor, Hawaii, on December 7, 1941.

Injured while storming Omaha Beach during the Normandy landings, American assault troops of the 16th Infantry Regiment wait to be taken to a field hospital on June 6, 1944.

representatives of the "Big Four"—the U.S., Britain, the USSR, and China—signed a Declaration of the United Nations (UN) based on the Atlantic Charter; a further twenty-two nations signed the following day.

There followed more than two years of grueling campaigns to liberate North Africa and Italy before Operation Overlord—the D-Day landings in Normandy, France, on June 6, 1944—marked the turning point in the war. The Allies' long-planned operation to liberate Western Europe was the largest amphibious assault ever launched and involved over 7,000 ships and around 11,000 aircraft. The Allies reached the German frontier in early September, and although a hard winter of fighting followed, the war in Europe ended with the acceptance of Germany's surrender on May 8, 1945; Italy had already surrendered, in September 1943. Japan ignored an ultimatum to surrender on July 28, 1945, and on August 6 the U.S. dropped an atomic bomb on Hiroshima, followed by a second on Nagasaki on August 9. Japan surrendered on August 15. The Manhattan Project, the research project that produced the bombs, was initiated in 1942 and involved high-profile physicists including Albert Einstein, who suggested its development, and J. Robert Oppenheimer.

In 1945, the UN was established formally at the United Nations Conference on International Organization, held in San Francisco. However, a new rivalry had already begun between the U.S. and the USSR, which became known as the Cold War. While the Allied forces were closing in on Germany from the west in 1945, the USSR's Red Army was closing in from the east to liberate Eastern Europe, Germany having reneged on its nonaggression pact with the USSR and invaded in 1941. After the war, the USSR wished to maintain control of Eastern Europe and further extend the communist ideology. The U.S. implemented various measures to contain the worldwide spread of communism, notably the Truman Doctrine, which offered aid to any nation considered under threat from Soviet expansionism, and the "Marshall Plan," a west- and south-European economic recovery program under U.S. sponsorship.

Between 1948 and 1949, the USSR made an unsuccessful attempt to blockade West Berlin, and in response the U.S. and its European allies formed the North Atlantic Treaty Organization (NATO) in 1949. Also that year, the USSR detonated its first atomic bomb, triggering the Nuclear Arms Race. In 1952, the U.S. tested the first hydrogen bomb on Bikini Atoll, its nuclear test site in the Pacific Marshall Islands, which in 2010 was inscribed a World Heritage Site. In 1954, the U.S. Secretary of State announced a "massive retaliation" policy, under which the U.S. would respond to any Soviet attack with a massive nuclear response, and both sides developed a land-based intercontinental ballistic missile, with a range of over 3,500 miles.

In 1961, the Soviets erected the Berlin Wall to contain the exodus from East Germany to the West, and in 1962 they began to install nuclear-armed missiles in Cuba, which President Kennedy concluded was in preparation for another takeover attempt on West Berlin, having been warned by the Soviet premier, Nikita Khrushchev, that this was his intention. Kennedy had warned that if the Soviets introduced offensive weapons in Cuba, "the gravest issues would arise." The Cuban Missile Crisis brought the U.S. and USSR to the brink of nuclear war; however, the crisis ended in a series of agreements between Kennedy and Khrushchev, and in 1963, the U.S., USSR, and Britain signed a Nuclear Test-Ban Treaty. Meanwhile, a Cold War space race was also underway—in 1961, the Soviet cosmonaut Yuri Gagarin became the first human to travel in space, and in 1969 the U.S. astronaut Neil Armstrong became the first person to walk on the moon.

Apollo 11 lifts off from the Kennedy Space Center in Florida and four days later, on July 20, 1969, becomes the first spaceflight to land humans on the moon.
It is piloted by Michael Collins and carries astronauts Neil Armstrong and Edwin "Buzz" Aldrin Jr.

In 1972 and 1979, the U.S. and the USSR signed SALT I and II, agreements arising from two series of Strategic Arms Limitation Talks. Congress did not ratify SALT II because the USSR invaded Afghanistan in 1980; however, negotiations were resumed in 1982 as the Strategic Arms Reduction Talks (START). The Cold War came to an end with the fall of communist regimes in 1989–90, the rise to power of democratic governments in East Germany, Poland, Hungary, and Czechoslovakia, the unification of East and West Germany, and, in 1991, the collapse of the Soviet Union.

In the years between the start of the Cold War and the fall of the Berlin Wall in 1990, the world had changed beyond recognition.

THE AMERICAN DREAM

The historian James Truslow Adams wrote in *The Epic of America* (1931) about the American Dream, "that dream of a land in which life should be better and richer and fuller for everyone, with opportunity for each according to ability or achievement." The decades following the end of World War II saw that opportunity opening up for many who were able to realize their dreams. For some, the dream was of material wealth; for others, of freedom from discrimination or social conventions.

The lingering hardships of the Great Depression came to an end during the war. By 1940, unemployment had dropped from 25 percent to 14.6 percent under FDR's New Deal measures; by 1950, it stood at a mere 5 percent. Between 1939 and the end of the war, membership of the U.S. armed forces rose from a peacekeeping 186,000 to around 15 million, while the demand for munitions created factory employment for millions more, with the U.S. supplying around two-thirds of the Allied forces' military equipment. The Servicemen's Readjustment Act (1944), commonly known at the G.I. Bill, provided an education and training program, low-interest mortgages and small-business loans, hiring

Senator John F. Kennedy and his wife, Jackie, wave from the back of a convertible in Massachusetts, shortly after his acceptance of the Democratic Party nomination for president of the United States in July 1960.

privileges, and unemployment compensation for returning veterans; many opted to participate in education or training, reducing job competition in the immediate postwar period while producing a newly skilled workforce. Congress, meanwhile, focused on creating a healthy economy; the Employment Act (1946) established a Council of Economic Advisors to President Truman and stated the government's responsibility for maintaining full employment.

America's gross national product (GNP) more than doubled in the 1950s, and doubled again in the 1960s; around two-thirds of Americans acquired the financial status of the middle class and, within a short time, most "ordinary" families owned a house, a car, a TV, a refrigerator—the consumer goods they had dreamed of since the Wall Street Crash. During the 1950s, Americans purchased nearly 60 million cars, facilitating the migration out of overcrowded urban centers into pleasant suburbs. Even farmers, formerly the poor relations, now flourished; the harsh lessons of the 1920s had been learned, and price controls to balance supply and demand remained in place after the war, while relief programs such as the United Nations Relief and Rehabilitation Administration and the subsequent Marshall Plan served as an effective export subsidy.

Consumerism was promoted on television. This new means of visual communication, owned by more than 90 percent of American households, also brought into American homes the shocking news of the assassination of President John F. Kennedy on November 22, 1963. Kennedy was by no means the first president to be assassinated, but he was the youngest man elected president, the youngest to die, and the first to die in an era when technology enabled constant live coverage of breaking news; TV commercials were suspended for the four days between his death and funeral. In the short time since he had taken office in January 1960, Kennedy had not only averted the Cuban Missile Crisis, which brought the world to the brink of nuclear war, but also launched programs for sustained economic expansion and to bring relief to areas where poverty persisted. His funeral on November 25 was broadcast live on TV and watched by millions; more than fifty years later, millions still remember exactly where they were when they heard that JFK had been shot. A second presidential shock came in 1974, when President Richard Nixon—faced with an impeachment trial over a scandal arising from a burglary by a Nixon-support group in the offices of the Democratic National Committee in Watergate—broke the news to the nation of his decision to resign in a TV broadcast on August 8, 1974. To date, Nixon is the only president to have resigned.

In much the same way as the Roaring Twenties inspired young Americans to adopt wild new crazes in fashion, music, and dancing, so too did the years after World War II. Rock 'n' roll was the new music, swing the dance to go with it;

a novel by Jack Kerouac

ON THE ROAD

girls wore circle skirts with layers of petticoats beneath, as much to celebrate the end of wartime fabric rationing as to facilitate the dance moves, while rebellious boys, as portrayed by James Dean in *Rebel Without a Cause* (1955), drove hot-rods and wore jeans and slicked-back hairstyles. Meanwhile, intellectuals embraced the cultural and literary Beat Movement in bohemian centers such as New York's Greenwich Village; core members included Jack Kerouac and Allen Ginsberg, who are credited with starting the movement at Columbia University in the 1940s, and John Clellon Holmes, whose book *Go* (1952) is considered the first Beat novel. "Beatniks" were anti-establishment, and considered everyday American society to be "square"; they rejected materialism, and adopted nonconformist styles of dress, a hip vocabulary, and Eastern religions. The Beat Generation inspired the emergence in the 1960s and 1970s of the "hippie" counterculture, also characterized by a rejection of materialism. Hippies, too, adopted an unconventional lifestyle; however, unlike beatniks, who favored jazz and somber black clothing, hippies favored folk music and flamboyant outfits in psychedelic colors, and their focus was on

During Operation Yellowstone, a few members of Company A, 3rd Battalion, 22nd Infantry (Mechanized), 25th Infantry Division, sing around a guitar after a difficult day in Vietnam (c. January 18–19, 1968).

promoting peace and love rather than intellectual debate. In 1967, a huge gathering of hippie "flower children," known as the Summer of Love, took place in San Francisco's Haight-Ashbury district. Two years later, another iconic event of the hippie era, the Woodstock Festival, was held in Woodstock, New York. The modern drug culture evolved from this period, with both beatniks and hippies experimenting with hallucinogenics as a way to expand spiritual consciousness.

The hippie movement was not merely an expression of self-indulgence, however—much of their philosophy was prompted by current affairs in the U.S. The Cold War and the containment of communism underpinned much of the second half of the twentieth century, leading to U.S. involvement in both the Korean War (1950–53), fought to halt the invasion by the Soviet-backed North Korean People's Army into U.S.-backed South Korea, and the more prolonged Vietnam War (1965–73), again between the communist North supported by the USSR and the South supported by the U.S. Meanwhile, a second Red Scare arose in the U.S. from an accusation by Senator Joseph McCarthy of covert communist activity taking place in government and public life, which led in the early 1950s to "McCarthyism," a paranoid hunt for infiltrators. Suspects found guilty were charged with subversion, since communism was not illegal. In 1954, McCarthy was censured by his colleagues and replaced as chairman of the Senate Permanent Subcommittee on Investigations. The House Un-American Activities Committee, established in 1938, also conducted investigations into alleged communist activities throughout the 1940s and 50s, targeting artists and entertainers in particular.

The Gay Liberation Movement gathered momentum from 1950, when the activist Harry Hay founded the Mattachine Society, the first national gay rights organization, with the aim of changing public perceptions of homosexuality; however, McCarthyism coincided with a persecution of homosexuals known as the "Lavender Scare." A 1950 Senate report entitled "Employment of Homosexuals and Other Sex Perverts in Government" defined homosexuality as a mental illness and stated that homosexuals constituted a security risk to the nation because the "lack of emotional stability which is found in most sex perverts, and the weakness of their moral fiber, makes them susceptible to the blandishments of the foreign espionage agent." Homosexuality remained on the American Psychiatric Association's list of mental illnesses as a "sociopathic personality disturbance" until 1973. The movement persisted

Photographer Diana Davies depicts the Greenwich Village gay bar the Stonewall Inn, which was raided by police on June 27, 1969, resulting in riots that furthered the gay liberation movement.

nonetheless, and the landmark case of *One, Inc. v. Olesen* in 1958, in which the Supreme Court ruled in favor of the pro-gay *One* magazine, was an unprecedented victory for the Gay Rights Movement. In 1969, a police raid on the Stonewall Inn, a gay bar in Greenwich Village, New York City, led to riots, inspiring the formation of Lesbian, Gay, Bisexual, and Transgender (LGBT) rights organizations in major cities throughout the U.S. The following year, a march through Central Park in commemoration of the riots was attended by thousands, and heralded the establishment of New York City's annual Gay Pride Week. The campaign to outlaw discrimination on the basis of sexual orientation is ongoing, with state laws varying widely.

The postwar years also saw the resurgence in the South of the Ku Klux Klan, who engaged in terrorist activities against the black community including lynching, bombing, whipping, and shooting. The revival was triggered by the emergence of the African American Civil Rights Movement. After the abolition of slavery in 1865, a series of laws was passed, requiring the separation of whites from "persons of color" in public transportation, schools, theaters, restaurants, parks, and even cemeteries. These became known as "Jim Crow" laws, named for a minstrel routine performed by the actor Thomas Dartmouth Rice in the mid 1800s. The "separate but equal" doctrine that rendered the laws constitutional theoretically, provided separate facilities for African Americans, although in practice the facilities were inferior on nonexistent. On public transportation, black passengers were allocated seating in the back half of the bus; but if there were insufficient seats for white passengers, black passengers were requested to move further back. On December 1, 1955, Rosa Parks—a member, along with her husband, of the Montgomery, Alabama, chapter of the National Association for the Advancement of Colored People—was arrested for refusing to give up her seat for a white passenger. This event, on "a day like any other day," led to a highly successful boycott of Montgomery's buses, organized by Dr. Martin Luther King Jr. and Ralph

Abernathy. In 1957, the two activists formed the Southern Christian Leadership Conference (SCLC), dedicated to bringing an end to segregation through nonviolent resistance. On August 28, 1963, Martin Luther King delivered his famous "I Have a Dream" speech from the steps of Washington's Lincoln Memorial. The following year, Congress passed the Civil Rights Act, which guaranteed equal voting rights and banned segregation and discrimination based on race, color, religion, or national origin, the culmination of a centuries-long struggle. King was awarded the Nobel Peace Prize in 1964; on April 4, 1968, he was assassinated by a white racist, James Earl Ray.

As the new millennium approached, a number of bizarre doomsday cults emerged around the world. However, despite dire predictions of the impending Apocalypse, the New Year's Eve ball dropped to an enthusiastic countdown in New York's Times Square as it had done every year since 1907, and the world awoke as usual on January 1, 2000, bringing new challenges for the United States.

Civil rights leader Martin Luther King Jr. gives his "I Have a Dream" speech to the crowd gathered at the Lincoln Memorial in Washington, D.C., during the March on Washington on August 28, 1963.

THE NEW MILLENNIUM

The twenty-first century has presented the United States with a series of challenges, the greatest being the terrorist attacks carried out by militant Islamic fundamentalists on the morning of September 11, 2001. For the first time since the assassination of John F. Kennedy in 1963, TV commercials were suspended as live coverage was broadcast of the devastation caused when the four hijacked commercial airlines slammed into the World Trade Center's 110-story-high Twin Towers, the Pentagon, and a field in Shanksville, Pennsylvania. It was not the first attack on the World Trade Center—in 1993, terrorists detonated a huge homemade bomb in a rental van parked beneath the North Tower. The National September 11 Memorial, opened on the site of the Twin Towers on the tenth anniversary of their destruction, commemorates both the six people killed on that occasion and the nearly 3,000 people killed in the 9/11 attacks and in the massive rescue operation that

This photograph of the Twin Towers of the World Trade Center in New York City was taken one month before the terrorist attacks on September 11, 2001.

followed; their names are inscribed on bronze panels edging twin Memorial pools. In addition to the Americans in the towers, there were workers from the UK, Japan, Ireland, Australia, New Zealand, Switzerland, India, Mexico, Brazil, South Africa, and Canada. A museum on the site, with exhibitions and artifacts relating to the 9/11 tragedy, incorporates features from the original towers such as the Vesey Street "Survivors' Stairs" used by survivors of the attack to escape.

Following the attacks, President George W. Bush immediately declared the "war on terror" that characterized the first decade of the century. Evidence indicated that the Islamic extremist organization al-Qaeda was responsible for 9/11, with the ultimate aim, according to one of the group's military commanders, of provoking the U.S. into making "serious and . . . fatal mistakes." The ruling Taliban militia in Afghanistan refused to extradite the group's leader, Osama

bin Laden, who had his headquarters there, and for the first time in history, NATO invoked Article 5 of the Washington Treaty (1949), which allows its members to respond collectively in self-defense, stating that the ultimate aim was "to restore and maintain the security of the North Atlantic area." On October 7, U.S. and allied forces launched Operation Enduring Freedom, the first attack in the Afghan War. Taliban power came to an end in December with the fall of Kandahar, the group's spiritual home. It was decided to hold prisoners at a detention camp in Guantánamo Bay, which the U.S. had leased from Cuba in 1903; Khalid Sheikh Mohammed, who masterminded the 9/11 attacks, was detained there from 2006. The second phase of the war, between 2002 and 2008, focused first on reconstruction and later on subduing Taliban resurgence; the third phase increased the troop presence to protect the country from the Taliban. U.S. Intelligence eventually located Osama bin Laden hiding out in a secure compound in Pakistan; he was killed by U.S. Navy SEALs on May 2, 2011.

Various other measures were taken in the aftermath Homeland Security and Homeland Security Council were established; both were superseded in January 2003 by the Department of Homeland Security. The USA Patriot Act (2001)—an acronym for Uniting and Strengthening America by Providing Appropriate Tools Required to Intercept and Obstruct Terrorism—was passed to increase the government's surveillance powers in the areas of records searches, secret searches, intelligence searches, and "trap and trace" searches.

On March 19, 2003, President Bush announced to the nation the launch of Operation Iraqi Freedom, the next step in the war against terror. Although Iraq's dictator, Saddam

Hussein, had initiated a number of progressive policies during his early career as the country's deputy president, he had assumed a ruthless dictatorship from 1979. Between 1980 and 1988, Iraq was at war with neighboring Iran, a conflict in which the Western world indirectly supported Iraq by overlooking various violations of international law. However, a U.S.-led coalition intervened when Iraqi troops then invaded Kuwait in 1990 and ignored a UN deadline for withdrawal. A series of Iraqi violations were addressed during the 1990s, but soon after 9/11, the U.S. received intelligence that Iraq was planning to launch its own attacks, and was also believed to be developing weapons of mass destruction in direct violation of the UN ceasefire agreement that had ended the 1990–91 Gulf War. The controversial invasion of Iraq by a U.S.-led coalition began on March 20, 2003, and Baghdad fell on April 9. Saddam was captured in December 2003, stood trial for crimes against humanity, and was executed on December 31, 2006. U.S. troops remained in Iraq to assist with continued attacks by insurgents. In 2009, Iraqi troops assumed responsibility for security operations and in September 2010, Operation Iraqi Freedom was renamed Operation New Dawn to reflect the U.S. troops' role change to an advisory and training capacity. U.S. involvement in Iraq officially ended on December 15, 2011.

There have been other disasters for America to mourn since the new millennium began. In 2003, the space shuttle *Columbia* exploded upon re-entry over Texas, killing its

During Operation Iraqi Freedom, U.S. troops enter central Baghdad's Firdaus Square and tear down a statue of President Saddam Hussein on April 9, 2003.

seven-member crew. *Columbia* had flown twenty-seven successful missions since becoming the first space shuttle to reach orbit in 1981. Between August 23 and 30, 2005, the tropical cyclone Hurricane Katrina struck the southeastern U.S., affecting Louisiana—especially New Orleans, which was devastated when its flood protection system failed—and, to a lesser extent, Mississippi. At the time, it was the largest hurricane ever recorded to make landfall in the U.S., and,

Photographer Liz Roll shows the devastating floodwaters in New Orleans, Louisiana, following Hurricane Katrina in 2005.

with a death toll of 1,836, the third deadliest, exceeded only by the Great Galveston Hurricane in 1900 (estimated death toll 8,000–12,000) and the Okeechobee Hurricane in 1928 (2,500–3,000). It was also the costliest, causing $81 billion worth of property damages alone; in addition to countless homes and many landmark historic buildings. In 2012, Katrina lost its status as the largest hurricane to 1,100-mile-diameter Sandy, which caused an estimated $65.6 billion worth of damage in the New York area and New Jersey. The Gulf of Mexico was also the location for a second disaster on April 20, 2010, when the BP Oil Company's Deepwater Horizon oil rig exploded and sank, killing eleven people. Caused by a surge of natural gas, the accident created the largest oil spill

Edie Windsor leaves the Supreme Court in Washington, D.C., on March 27, 2013, after challenging the constitutionality of Section 3 of the Defense of Marriage act (DOMA) during the landmark case *United States v. Windsor*.

in history, estimated at well over 100 million gallons. The well was announced sealed on September 19, but an estimated 1,100 miles of shoreline were polluted by the spill, decimating wildlife, fouling marshes and wetlands, and shutting down businesses.

Meanwhile, in 2007, the U.S. experienced an economic downturn on a par with the Great Depression. It was by no means the first recession since the 1929 Wall Street Crash—in fact, one of the worst was in 1937–38, with further recessions of varying length and severity occurring throughout the rest of the twentieth century—but it would be the longest and, with the exception of the brief postwar recession in 1945, have the greatest impact on gross domestic product (GDP) since the 1930s. The Great Recession of 2008 was prompted by a crash in house prices in 2007, caused by the issuing of subprime mortgages, which typically carry higher than average interest rates to offset risk. The result was the same as the 1926 house-price crash, leaving subprime mortgage-holders in a state of negative equity and defaulting on their loans, which were often funded by borrowing on equity. This in turn had a severe impact on the financial market, affecting mortgage lenders, including the nation's largest, Countrywide Financial Corp.; insurers, including the largest, American International Group (AIG); and investment banks, most notably the fourth-largest, Lehman

Brothers, which collapsed and filed for bankruptcy on September 15, 2008. The Emergency Economic Stabilization Act (2008) created the Office of Financial Stability to administer the Troubled Asset Relief Program (TARP), which provided federal aid for buyout and bailout operations, while the Dodd-Frank Wall Street Reform Act was passed in 2010 to regulate banking practices.

The financial market was not the only industry affected by the Great Recession; the huge U.S. auto industry also suffered, with both Chrysler and General Motors declaring bankruptcy in 2009, and many other businesses failed as lenders were unwilling to extend credit. The problem of rising unemployment was addressed by the American Recovery and Reinvestment Act (ARRA, 2009), passed to save existing jobs and create new ones. However, the financial crisis prompted the formation in 2009 of the populist "Tea Party" movement to protest excessive taxation and government intervention in the private sector—"TEA" both references the causes of the 1773 Boston Tea Party and serves as an acronym for "Taxed Enough Already." In the 2010 midterm elections, a number of Tea Party-affiliated candidates won Republican nominations, possibly contributing to the Republicans' success that saw the party reduce the Democratic majority in the Senate and, more importantly, regain control of the House of Representatives. In 2013, this led to a three-week government shutdown over Obamacare which the Republican-led House had repeatedly voted to repeal, defund, or delay. The shutdown soon turned into a debt-ceiling crisis—on October 17, the Treasury would reach the limits of its borrowing power, putting the U.S. at risk of defaulting on its debts. Agreement with only hours to spare. Meanwhile, the 2011 Occupy Wall Street movement used the slogan "We are the 99%" to fight against income inequality.

Despite these and many other problems, there were advancements in social progress and civil rights. In 2010, the U.S. Navy lifted its ban of women in submarines. In 2013 the U.S. Supreme Court struck down Section 3 of the Defense of Marriage Act (DOMA), which defined "spouse" as pertaining only to marriage between a husband and wife, in the landmark case *United States v. Windsor*. The case arose after New York resident Edie Windsor faced $363,053 in estate taxes because she was barred from receiving the federal tax exemption for surviving spouses after inheriting the estate of her partner Thea Spyer, whom she had been in a relationship with for more than forty years and legally married in Ontario, Canada, in 2007. However, for many Americans and non-Americans, one date stands out as testimony to how far the U.S. has come since the early days of the colonists: November 4, 2008, the day Barack Obama became the first African American president.

Science brought us closer to understanding ourselves and the universe around us. The Human Genome Project, an international biological research project that seeks to map out all the genes for complete genetic information for humans, was initially funded in the U.S. in 1987, and in 2003 a complete draft of the genome was announced. American Dennis Tito became the first space tourist when he funded his own trip aboard a Russian spacecraft. In 2004, the robotic rover Opportunity found evidence that part of Mars was once covered by water. By 2014, NASA publicized the discovery of more than a thousand confirmed exoplanets.

Today, tablet computers, phone apps, and E-commerce are mainstays. The Millennial Generation, the demographic born in the early 1980s to early 2000s, relies heavily on technology, such as using social-media sites like Facebook and Twitter. America's future may change with just a click of a button.

President-elect Barack Obama speaks at the "We Are One" Obama Inaugural Celebration at the Lincoln Memorial on Sunday, January 18, 2009.

America's Contribution to the World

America has contributed hugely to global evolution in the way of inventions, both large and small (coat hangers, pop-up toasters, and Post-it notes are among the nation's smaller but very significant offerings), but this still relatively young country has also done much else to inspire. The history of the United States, and its meteoric rise from a handful of humble colonies to a superpower, holds more fascination for people beyond its shores than that of any other nation, and here we take a brief look at what America has shared with the world.

Since the Industrial Revolution, the U.S. has achieved much in the way of technological advancement. In 1876, the Scottish-born inventor Alexander Graham Bell demonstrated his telephone at the Centennial Exposition in Philadelphia, initiating a new form of communication that others have since developed in many diverse ways, facilitated by complementary inventions such as Nikola Tesla's coil transformer (1891), Lee de Forest's triode vacuum tube for amplifying radio signals (1907), and Edwin Armstrong's superheterodyne circuit (1918) and frequency-modulated (FM) radio (1933). The Atanasoff-Berry computer, developed between 1939 and 1942, is credited as the first electronic digital computer; IBM, founded in Endicott, New York, in

Following Neil Armstrong, Edwin "Buzz" Aldrin walks on the Moon on July 21, 1969.

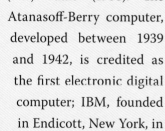

M001 is an early model of the Apple Macintosh computer (c. 1984).

1911, introduced the first mass-produced computer in 1953 and its first personal computer in 1981. In 1975, Bill Gates co-founded the computer software Microsoft Corporation and the following year Steve Jobs co-founded the hardware company, Apple Inc. The invention of the world wide web in 1989 and the development of the web browser Netscape, launched in 1995 by Marc Andreessen and the "Silicon Valley" technology entrepreneur James H. Clark, gave rise to the information technology revolution and the evolution of social networking services such as Facebook Inc., co-founded by Mark Zuckerberg in 2004. Clark's health and medical information website Healtheon, founded in 1996, would have been an unimaginable innovation to the American doctors Charles and William Mayo, co-founders in 1889 of the world-famous medical research group the Mayo Clinic, although Dr. Jonas Salk used technology— a national radio show, broadcast on March 26, 1953—to

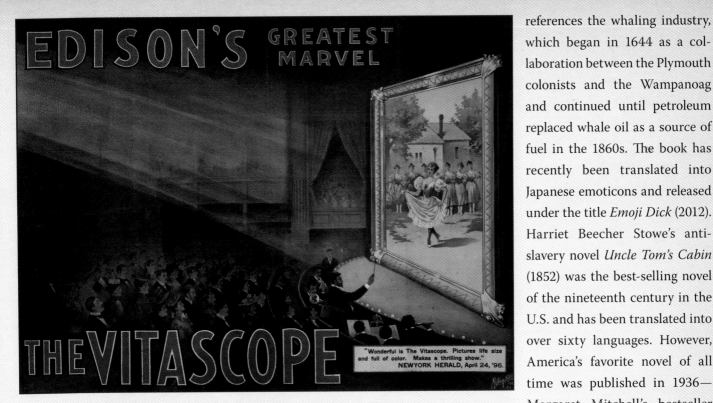

EDISON'S GREATEST MARVEL

THE VITASCOPE

"Wonderful is The Vitascope. Pictures life size and full of color. Makes a thrilling show."
NEW YORK HERALD, April 24, '96.

Manufactured by the Edison factory, the Vitascope was an early film projector.

announce his development of a vaccine against poliomyelitis, at that time a pandemic disease.

America has also led the way in space exploration since the foundation in 1958 of the National Aeronautics and Space Administration (NASA). Highlights of the space program to date range from the ground breaking Mercury and Gemini manned space programs to the secrets of the Universe revealed in the Hubble Space Telescope's awe-inspiring images. But to date the most memorable moment was on July 21, 1969, when the astronaut Neil Armstrong set foot on the moon and took "one giant leap for mankind."

Long before technology played a major part in everyday life, however, both Euro- and African-Americans portrayed their New World experiences through literature. In 1650, the English settler Anne Bradstreet became the first female writer to be published in the British colonies and the first poet published in both America and England. The "slave poet" Phillis Wheatley, famous for her 1768 poem "On being brought from Africa to America," was also published in both America and England. James Fenimore Cooper's *The Last of the Mohicans* (1826), set in the French and Indian War (1754–63), is one of the world's most widely read novels. Herman Melville's *Moby Dick* (1851)

references the whaling industry, which began in 1644 as a collaboration between the Plymouth colonists and the Wampanoag and continued until petroleum replaced whale oil as a source of fuel in the 1860s. The book has recently been translated into Japanese emoticons and released under the title *Emoji Dick* (2012). Harriet Beecher Stowe's anti-slavery novel *Uncle Tom's Cabin* (1852) was the best-selling novel of the nineteenth century in the U.S. and has been translated into over sixty languages. However, America's favorite novel of all time was published in 1936—Margaret Mitchell's bestseller *Gone With The Wind*, set in the Civil War, which won the 1937 Pulitzer Prize and has sold an estimated 30 million copies worldwide.

In 1939, *Gone With The Wind* was released as a movie and remained the No. 1 box-office hit until 1965, when it was overtaken by *The Sound of Music*. The history of the American film industry began in the late 1800s with a number of inventors developing movie cameras. These included Thomas Edison, who in 1891 patented his kinetograph using flexible film developed by George Eastman, inventor of the Kodak Brownie camera (1900). The world's first motion picture screening took place in 1896 at Koster & Bial's Music Hall in New York City, using a Vitascope, a projector patented by Thomas Armat of Washington, D.C., in 1895. The Los Angeles film industry began in 1902, with the

The Edison lab developed the first motion-picture camera, the kinetograph.

opening of the purpose-built Electric Theater; the first permanent film studio was established in 1907. The first film shot in Hollywood was *In Old California* (1910), directed by D. W. Griffith, whose 1915 film *The Birth of a Nation* introduced groundbreaking techniques such as story flashbacks, close-ups, and cross-cutting. The first Oscar awards ceremony was held in Hollywood in 1929; in 1953, NBC televised the Academy Awards for the first time and the event has been broadcast live internationally since 1969. Much of what the world knows about America's history has been gleaned from film and television; the language barrier was overcome early on by the technique of subtitling to enable foreign translations to appear on film—the first use was with *The Jazz Singer* (1927), the world's first feature-length talkie, which opened in Paris in 1929 with French subtitles.

The design of Thomas Edison's kinetograph was based on his earlier invention of the cylinder phonograph, patented in 1877. In 1887, the German-born American inventor Emile Berliner patented the first gramophone, which replaced Edison's cylinder design with a flat disc known as a "record." Early commercial recordings were mainly of classical music, but in 1917 the Original Dixieland Jass [*sic*] Band, a group of white musicians from New Orleans, the home of jazz,

recorded the first jazz record and first ever million-selling recording, "Livery Stable Blues." A number of white bands followed suit and recorded jazz music, bringing mainstream America into the Jazz Age of the 1920s; a notable bandleader was Paul Whiteman, the "King of Jazz," who in 1924 commissioned George Gershwin's famous *Rhapsody in Blue*.

However, an African American cultural movement known as the Harlem Renaissance was also underway at this time, with music underpinning the literature and art that flourished into the late 1930s. In 1920, the vaudeville singer Mamie Smith recorded "Crazy Blues"; the song sold more than a million copies in under a year and gave rise to "race records," a new market in blues, jazz, and gospel music recorded exclusively by African American musicians. Many of the big jazz names, such as Duke Ellington and Louis Armstrong, became famous in the 1920s, while two of the great female singers, Ella Fitzgerald and Billie Holiday, emerged in the 1930s. The genre became popular worldwide and today a number of annual jazz festivals are held, from the famous New Orleans Jazz and Heritage Festival to Denmark's Copenhagen Jazz Festival and Australia's Wangaratta Festival of Jazz and Blues. The "blues" also originated in the South, on the crop plantations in the Mississippi Delta where, after the Civil War, the practice of "sharecropping" evolved—in theory, landowners leased land to former slaves in return for a share of the crop, but in practice the sharecroppers often remained enslaved by indebtedness. Despite this, blues' lyrics are often

Left: *Down Beat* magazine features a photograph of jazz singer Billie Holiday (c. February 1947).

Above: Vaudeville singer Mamie Smith stands with Joseph Samuels' Jazz Band, which included Gavin Bushell, Herb Flemming, Everett Robbins, Julius Berkin, and Samuels.

Baseball fans waiting for the gates to open at Ebbets Field in Brooklyn on October 6, 1920, enjoy hot dogs.

full of wry humor and the term refers only to the musical "blue" notes that characterize the genre. While the blues spread north and entered into mainstream American music later than jazz, global aficionados are familiar with the 1920s bluesmen. Annual blues festivals are also held worldwide, from the festival in Chicago, the "Blues Capital of the World," to Poland's Suwalki Blues Festival and India's Mahindra Blues Festival.

It is not only American technology and culture that has spread, however; a number of U.S. activists have also influenced others. Although the African-American Civil Rights Movement was inspired in part by the Indian nationalist Mahatma Gandhi, who in 1893 refused to comply with South African racial segregation regulations, that country in turn was encouraged by the outcome of the act of civil disobedience in 1955 by Rosa Parks, who met Nelson Mandela in Detroit soon after his release from prison in 1990. The global Gay Rights Movement was inspired by the 1969 Stonewall Riots and the commemorative Gay Pride Parade, and Pride Parades are now held annually in cities including São Paulo (the world's largest), London, Tokyo, Tel Aviv, Berlin, Antwerp, Toronto, and Amsterdam as well as in New York City and other U.S. cities.

In more recent years, the effects of climate change have become an important issue, and in 2009 the environmentalist, activist, and author of *The End of Nature*, Bill McKibben, organized the International Day of Climate Action, a global one-day event to raise awareness of the need, identified by NASA, to decrease carbon dioxide concentration in the atmosphere to 350 parts per million. The number "three-fifty" was the focus of the day and activists in 181 countries found creative and often fitting ways to construct and display it, using anything from sandbags to solar ovens and even humans. The 350 Movement is ongoing and growing.

Often, though, it is simply the rhythms of everyday American life that intrigue the wider world, the remnants carried forward from life in the Old World combined with the mores that unite the modern United States. For example, the Amish community, which arrived in Pennsylvania from Europe in the 1730s, is perpetually fascinating for the old-fashioned traditions to which they adhere, such as appearance, mode of dress, and horse-drawn transport. The 1985 movie *Witness*, set in an Amish settlement, won two Academy awards; the set, in Lancaster County, became a popular tourist attraction. This, coupled with the popularity of the austere but beautifully crafted furniture inspired by the Shakers, or Shaking Quakers, who settled in America from England in 1774 under the leadership of Ann Lee (1736–84), suggest a yearning for a return to the simple life. At the other end of the scale, the thrills of the Super Bowl, which began in 1967, are enjoyed worldwide; many visitors to the U.S. consider attendance at a sporting event a must—and eating a hot dog, beloved since Charles Feltman opened the first stand in Brooklyn, NY, in 1867, is definitely another.

METRO BOOKS
New York

An Imprint of Sterling Publishing
387 Park Avenue South
New York, NY 10016

ISBN 978-1-4351-5393-6

For information about custom editions, special sales, and premium
and corporate purchases, please contact Sterling Special Sales at
800-8055489 or specialsales@sterlingpublishing.com.

Manufactured in China

2 4 6 8 10 9 7 5 3 1

www.sterlingpublishing.com

PHOTO CREDITS

INTRODUCTION: © mjbs/Thinkstock

NATIVE AMERICANS: © Los Angeles County Museum of Art/Art
Resource, NY: top; © Richard A. Cooke/Corbis: bottom left; Library of
Congress: bottom right

© Buffalo Bill Center of the West/The Art Archive/Art Resource,
NY: top left; National Archives: bottom left & top right; © Cardaf/
Shutterstock: bottom right

THE EXPLORERS: Courtesy Wikimedia Foundation/Metropolitan
Museum of Art: left; Library of Congress: right

Courtesy Wikimedia Foundation/Architect of the Capitol

THE COLONISTS: © akg-images: left; Library of Congress: right

© Marcio Jose Bastos Silva/Shutterstock: left; Courtesy Wikimedia
Foundation/Brooklyn Museum: right

THE WAR OF INDEPENDENCE: Photography by Christopher Bain/
Courtesy James C. Nannos Collection: left; Library of Congress: right

Yale University Art Gallery: left; Courtesy Wikimedia Foundation/
United States Capitol: right

THE INDUSTRIAL REVOLUTION: Library of Congress: left;
National Archives: right

Library of Congress: top left; © Underwood & Underwood/Corbis:
bottom left; Photography by Christopher Bain: top right; © Culver
Pictures/Art Resource, NY: bottom right

Library of Congress

WESTWARD EXPANSION: National Archives: top left; © Franz-Marc
Frei/Corbis: bottom left; Bridgeman Art Library: right

The Walters Art Museum: left; Library of Congress: top right; Courtesy
of the National Museum of American History/Smithsonian Institution:
bottom right

Horseshoe Canyon in Canyonlands National Park, Utah, contains one of North America's most important Native American works of rock art. In near perfect condition, the life-sized pictographs in the Great Gallery are estimated to be about 4,000 years old.

IN CONGRESS, JULY 4, 1776.

The unanimous Declaration of the thirteen united States of America,

When in the Course of human events it becomes necessary for one people to dissolve the political bands which have connected them with another, and to assume among the powers of the earth, the separate and equal station to which the Laws of Nature and of Nature's God entitle them, a decent respect to the opinions of mankind requires that they should declare the causes which impel them to the separation. ———— We hold these truths to be self-evident, that all men are created equal, that they are endowed by their Creator with certain unalienable Rights, that among these are Life, Liberty and the pursuit of Happiness. — That to secure these rights, Governments are instituted among Men, deriving their just powers from the consent of the governed, — That whenever any Form of Government becomes destructive of these ends, it is the Right of the People to alter or to abolish it, and to institute new Government, laying its foundation on such principles and organizing its powers in such form, as to them shall seem most likely to effect their Safety and Happiness. Prudence, indeed, will dictate that Governments long established should not be changed for light and transient causes; and accordingly all experience hath shewn, that mankind are more disposed to suffer, while evils are sufferable, than to right themselves by abolishing the forms to which they are accustomed. But when a long train of abuses and usurpations, pursuing invariably the same Object evinces a design to reduce them under absolute Despotism, it is their right, it is their duty, to throw off such Government, and to provide new Guards for their future security. — Such has been the patient sufferance of these Colonies; and such is now the necessity which constrains them to alter their former Systems of Government. The history of the present King of Great Britain is a history of repeated injuries and usurpations, all having in direct object the establishment of an absolute Tyranny over these States. To prove this, let Facts be submitted to a candid world. ———— He has refused his Assent to Laws, the most wholesome and necessary for the public good. ———— He has forbidden his Governors to pass Laws of immediate and pressing importance, unless suspended in their operation till his Assent should be obtained; and when so suspended, he has utterly neglected to attend to them. ———— He has refused to pass other Laws for the accommodation of large districts of people, unless those people would relinquish the right of Representation in the Legislature, a right inestimable to them and formidable to tyrants only. ———— He has called together legislative bodies at places unusual, uncomfortable, and distant from the depository of their public Records, for the sole purpose of fatiguing them into compliance with his measures. ———— He has dissolved Representative Houses repeatedly, for opposing with manly firmness his invasions on the rights of the people. ———— He has refused for a long time, after such dissolutions, to cause others to be elected; whereby the Legislative powers, incapable of Annihilation, have returned to the People at large for their exercise; the State remaining in the mean time exposed to all the dangers of invasion from without, and convulsions within. ———— He has endeavoured to prevent the population of these States; for that purpose obstructing the Laws for Naturalization of Foreigners; refusing to pass others to encourage their migrations hither, and raising the conditions of new Appropriations of Lands. ———— He has obstructed the Administration of Justice, by refusing his Assent to Laws for establishing Judiciary powers. ———— He has made Judges dependent on his Will alone, for the tenure of their offices, and the amount and payment of their salaries. ———— He has erected a multitude of New Offices, and sent hither swarms of Officers to harrass our people, and eat out their substance. ———— He has kept among us, in times of peace, Standing Armies without the Consent of our legislatures. ———— He has affected to render the Military independent of and superior to the Civil power. ———— He has combined with others to subject us to a jurisdiction foreign to our constitution, and unacknowledged by our laws; giving his Assent to their Acts of pretended Legislation: ———— For Quartering large bodies of armed troops among us: ———— For protecting them, by a mock Trial, from punishment for any Murders which they should commit on the Inhabitants of these States: ———— For cutting off our Trade with all parts of the world: ———— For imposing Taxes on us without our Consent: ———— For depriving us in many cases, of the benefits of Trial by jury: ———— For transporting us beyond Seas to be tried for pretended offences ———— For abolishing the free System of English Laws in a neighbouring Province, establishing therein an Arbitrary government, and enlarging its Boundaries so as to render it at once an example and fit instrument for introducing the same absolute rule into these Colonies: ———— For taking away our Charters, abolishing our most valuable Laws, and altering fundamentally the Forms of our Governments: ———— For suspending our own Legislatures, and declaring themselves invested with power to legislate for us in all cases whatsoever. ———— He has abdicated Government here, by declaring us out of his Protection and waging War against us. ———— He has plundered our seas, ravaged our Coasts, burnt our towns, and destroyed the lives of our people. ———— He is at this time transporting large Armies of foreign Mercenaries to compleat the works of death, desolation and tyranny, already begun with circumstances of Cruelty & perfidy scarcely paralleled in the most barbarous ages, and totally unworthy the Head of a civilized nation. ———— He has constrained our fellow Citizens taken Captive on the high Seas to bear Arms against their country, to become the executioners of their friends and Brethren, or to fall themselves by their Hands. ———— He has excited domestic insurrections amongst us, and has endeavoured to bring on the inhabitants of our frontiers, the merciless Indian Savages, whose known rule of warfare, is an undistinguished destruction of all ages, sexes and conditions. In every stage of these Oppressions We have Petitioned for Redress in the most humble terms: Our repeated Petitions have been answered only by repeated injury. A Prince, whose character is thus marked by every act which may define a Tyrant, is unfit to be the ruler of a free people. Nor have We been wanting in attentions to our British brethren. We have warned them from time to time of attempts by their legislature to extend an unwarrantable jurisdiction over us. We have reminded them of the circumstances of our emigration and settlement here. We have appealed to their native justice and magnanimity, and we have conjured them by the ties of our common kindred to disavow these usurpations, which, would inevitably interrupt our connections and correspondence. They too have been deaf to the voice of justice and of consanguinity. We must, therefore, acquiesce in the necessity, which denounces our Separation, and hold them, as we hold the rest of mankind, Enemies in War, in Peace Friends. ————

We, therefore, the Representatives of the united States of America, in General Congress, Assembled, appealing to the Supreme Judge of the world for the rectitude of our intentions, do, in the Name, and by Authority of the good People of these Colonies, solemnly publish and declare, That these United Colonies are, and of Right ought to be Free and Independent States; that they are Absolved from all Allegiance to the British Crown, and that all political connection between them and the State of Great Britain, is and ought to be totally dissolved; and that as Free and Independent States, they have full Power to levy War, conclude Peace, contract Alliances, establish Commerce, and to do all other Acts and Things which Independent States may of right do. ———— And for the support of this Declaration, with a firm reliance on the protection of divine Providence, we mutually pledge to each other our Lives, our Fortunes and our sacred Honor.

John Hancock

Button Gwinnett
Lyman Hall
Geo Walton.

Wm Hooper
Joseph Hewes,
John Penn

Edward Rutledge.

Thos Heyward Junr.
Thomas Lynch Junr.
Arthur Middleton

Samuel Chase
Wm Paca
Thos Stone
Charles Carroll of Carrollton

George Wythe
Richard Henry Lee
Th Jefferson
Benja Harrison
Thos Nelson jr.
Francis Lightfoot Lee
Carter Braxton

Robt Morris
Benjamin Rush
Benja Franklin
John Morton
Geo Clymer
Jas Smith
Geo Taylor
James Wilson
Geo. Ross
Caesar Rodney
Geo Read
Tho M:Kean

Wm Floyd
Phil. Livingston
Frans Lewis
Lewis Morris

Richd Stockton
Jno Witherspoon
Fras Hopkinson
John Hart
Abra Clark

Josiah Bartlett
Wm Whipple
Saml Adams
John Adams
Robt Treat Paine
Elbridge Gerry
Step Hopkins
William Ellery
Roger Sherman
Saml Huntington
Wm Williams
Oliver Wolcott
Matthew Thornton